THE ADVENTURE OF THE CRYSTAL WARRIOR

The view over the barrel of the autoelectromag (AEM) is a heavy drift of wet snow with green stalks futilely striving ... mp of irises, crushed by the snow, is the tar... feels unconditional love for the Earth w... shooting outward from the crystal in th... ergy of the Earth flowing up from the g... energy of the universe courses down thr... of energy reaches the roots at the base of ... ...g energy spins downward through the plant ... .jc jorce of the Earth, then spirals upwards seeking the sun. W ... vision of the healthy blooming flowers completely forms in the operator's mind, the healing of the plant is accomplished.

Crystal Warrior continues the adventure started in *Crystal Power* and *Crystal Spirit*, exploring the understanding and practical use of crystal energies. Since *Crystal Power* was published in 1985, one of the most common requests has been, "How can I obtain or build an autoelectromag (AEM)?" An AEM is an energy projector that combines black box psionics with the use of crystals to further your ability to create a better reality. Now, for the first time anywhere, this book explores the evolution of AEMs from weapons to tools for spiritual development and gives detailed instructions for building and using these tools.

The crystal warrior is, in essence, weaponless since the warrior does not see a hostile world and the possibility of meeting an enemy. What other people perceive as weapons—a crystal knife, crystal sword or crystal projector—the warrior sees as tools for meeting with and exploring other aspects of self. When a person is on the path of the crystal warrior, all battles are within, on a mental, emotional or spiritual plane.

The AEM may be the weapon of the future that shapes our world into one of peace and spiritual harmony. Once we realize that our enemies are merely the reflections of our own disordered thoughts, it will be possible to love these reflections of ourselves and live in harmony with them. With the help of crystal tools, we will come to the realization that we are the embodiment of the Earth energy, and we'll discover that balanced energy provides the key to ourselves and our personal transformation. When we've accomplished this, we can progress to higher-level spiritual challenges that preclude war and strife. Only then will we realize our full potential as Children of the Light.

The path of the crystal warrior leads from ourselves to the Earth and back again with a whole new attitude for living a healthy, powerful and balanced life. We hope you enjoy the adventure.

ABOUT THE AUTHORS

Michael G. Smith was born in Great Bend, Kansas on March 9, 1947. He has studied ancient knowledge for 28 years and spent time in the 1970s with the Bear Tribe Medicine Society, where he was first introduced to quartz crystals. This inspired Michael to invent the crystal healing rod. Several years later, he decided to combine the energy of crystals with the psionic black box, and the autoelectromags were born. In addition to writing and working for a Denver electronics firm, Michael is currently experimenting with the use of electricity to further boost the power of the autoelectromags.

Lin Westhorp was born of American military parents on March 9, 1949 in Frankfurt, Germany. In her teens and twenties, after being thrust into the world of the occult by a series of mystical experiences, she began exploring ESP, astrology, numerology, and reincarnation. She was introduced to channeling and new age philosophy in the late seventies, and her personal channeling questions resulted in the prediction of her meeting, marriage to, and work with Michael Smith. Their meeting was the catalyst to what she had always known would be her life's work—writing.

TO WRITE TO THE AUTHORS

If you wish to contact the author or would like more information about this book, please write to the author in care of Llewellyn Worldwide and we will forward your request. Both the author and publisher appreciate hearing from you and learning of your enjoyment of this book and how it has helped you. Llewellyn Worldwide cannot guarantee that every letter written to the author can be answered, but all will be forwarded. Please write to:

Michael G. Smith & Lin Westhorp
c/o Llewellyn Worldwide
P.O. Box 64383-727, St. Paul, MN 55164-0383, U.S.A.

Please enclose a self-addressed, stamped envelope for reply, or $1.00 to cover costs.
If outside the U.S.A., enclose international postal reply coupon.

FREE CATALOG FROM LLEWELLYN

For more than 90 years Llewellyn has brought its readers knowledge in the fields of metaphysics and human potential. Learn about the newest books in spiritual guidance, natural healing, astrology, occult philosophy and more. Enjoy book reviews, new age articles, a calendar of events, plus current advertised products and services. To get your free copy of *Llewellyn's New Worlds of Mind and Spirit*, send your name and address to:

Llewellyn's New Worlds of Mind and Spirit
P.O. Box 64383-727, St. Paul, MN 55164-0383, U.S.A.

CRYSTAL WARRIOR

Shamanic Transformation &
Projection of Universal Energy

Michael G. Smith & Lin Westhorp

Distributed by:
W. FOULSHAM & CO. LTD.,
YEOVIL ROAD, SLOUGH, SL1 4JH ENGLAND

Crystal Warrior. Copyright © 1992 by Michael G. Smith and Lin Westhorp. All rights reserved. Printed in the United States of America. No part of this book may be used or reproduced in any manner whatsoever without permission in writing from Llewellyn Publications except in the case of brief quotations embodied in critical articles and reviews.

FIRST EDITION, 1992
First Printing, 1992

Cover painting by Randy Asplund-Faith
Illustrations by Charles Smith
Photographs by J.J. Gauthier

Library of Congress Cataloging-in-Publication Data

Smith, Michael G. (Michael Gary), 1947–
  Crystal warrior : shamanic transformation & projection of universal energy / Michael G. Smith & Lin Westhorp.
     p.   cm.
  ISBN 0-87542-727-8
  1. Crystals—Psychic aspects. 2. Magic—Equipment and supplies.
  I. Westhorp, Lin, 1949– . II. Title.
BF1442.C78S656   1992
133—dc20
                                                            92-31533
                                                               CIP

Llewellyn Publications
A Division of Llewellyn Worldwide, Ltd.
P.O. Box 64383, St. Paul, MN 55164-0383

DEDICATED TO

Those who are building a world of peace and love

Other Books by Michael G. Smith
Crystal Power (Llewellyn Publications)
Crystal Spirit (Llewellyn Publications)

Forthcoming by Michael G. Smith
Quality in Your Life
Black Dog Moon

Forthcoming by Lin Westhorp
Crystal Trails
Open Doorways
An Organic Gardening Workbook
Fatal Prophecy

CONTENTS

Foreword xi

Introduction xiii

PART I   SHAMAN AND WARRIOR 1

    Chapter 1   The Modern Shaman 3
                      The Magic Circle 5

    Chapter 2   The Crystal Warrior 7

    Chapter 3   The Crystal Warrior's Weapons 13

    Chapter 4   The Inner Battle 17

    Chapter 5   Autoelectromag (AEM) 19
                      What Is the Autoelctromag or AEM? ... 19
                      The Principle Behind the AEM 20
                      The AEM as a Tool of Change 23
                      Turning Guns into Spiritual Projectors .. 23
                      Using the Autoelectromags 25
                      Summary of Operating Procedures 27
                      Description of Practice 28

    Chapter 6   Autoelectromag (AEM) I 33
                      The Earth Is a Reflection of Ourselves ... 33
                      Preparing for AEM Use 35
                      Psi-Sub AEM 35
                      AEM Beamer 42

    Chapter 7   Autoelectromag (AEM) II 47
                      Space Age Autoelectromag 47
                      X-Tal Autoelectromag 55
                      Mini Autoelectromag 59
                      Crystal Amplifier for Mini AEM 62

PART II OTHER MAGICAL WEAPONS AND TOOLS ... 65

Chapter 8	Ancient Crystal Weapons 71	
	A Memory: The Outlands of Atlantis ... 72	
	Recalling Our Past Lives 73	
	Crystal Blade Rod 74	
	Crystal Battle-Axe 78	
	Crystal War Club 80	
	Crystal Scepter 80	
Chapter 9	Crystal Swords and Dagger 85	
	Full Size Crystal Swords 86	
	Two Crystal Wooden Swords from One 90	
	Crystal Excalibur Short Sword 96	
	Crystal Dagger 96	
Chapter 10	Crystal Self-Defense Sticks 101	
	Special Crystal Defense Stick 103	
	Suggested Uses for Crystal Defense Sticks 104	
Chapter 11	Aura Amplifiers and Accessories 107	
	Aura Amplifiers 107	
	Crystal and Leather Accessories 111	
	Aural Headband 111	
	Warrior Armband 115	
	Amazon Anklet or Choker 118	
	Mystic Gauntlets and Other Accessories 121	
	Crystal Mask 121	
	Metal and Crystal Accessories 124	
	Power Wristbands 124	
	Energy Bracelets 127	

PART III EARTH ENERGIES 129

Chapter 12	Crystal Garden and Crystal Arranging ... 131	
	Crystal Rock Garden 131	
	Crystal and Rock Arranging 134	
Chapter 13	Crystal Jewelry 139	
	Jewelry Making 141	

Chapter 14	Aggressive and Household Shields 143
	Aggressive Shield 143
	Household Shield 147
Chapter 15	Crystal Water of Life 151
	Nion Generator 152
	The Benefits of Negative Ions 154
	Suggested Uses for Crystal Water of Life 154
	Simple Crystal-Charged Water 157
Chapter 16	The Power and the Spirit 159
	Healing Circle—The Pipe Ceremony . . 160
	Spiritual Healing 162
	Final Words 163
	Channeled Message 165
Appendix A	New Rods for the Nineties 167
	Wooden Crystal Rods 167
	Single and Double Wooden Rods 168
	Crystal Spike Rods 172
	Triple Crystal Spike Rod 173
	Container Crystal Rod with Handguard 176
	Extension Rods 177
	Crystal Squeeze and Penlight Rods 180
Appendix B	Piezo Rods and Crystal Frivolities 183
	Piezo Crystal Rods 183
	Leifheit Model 184
	Piezo Igniter Crystal Rod 184
	Crystal Frivolities 187
	Crystal Pens, Pointers, Razors, Combs and Toothbrushes 188
	Crystal Umbrella 190
	Crystal Canes 191
	Crystal Bullwhip 194
	Crystal Riding Crop 194

Foreword

The spirit of the crystal warrior is the channel of life.

Crystal Warrior has been described by some as the book that should never have been written. We've been told that there are crystal tools of self-development that shouldn't be placed in the hands of the people. Of course, the same was said of the other two books in the crystal trilogy (*Crystal Power* and *Crystal Spirit*). We put off writing this book for a long time, even though it contains information that crystal workers around the world have asked for. But *now* the time is right, and we are making these tools available to anyone who reads *Crystal Warrior*.

It's ironic that the biggest block to writing this book has been due to an unspoken rule. The rule appears to be, "Don't introduce anything new into the New Age!" Our success in crystal research and crystal inventions has been due to constantly breaking the unspoken rule as you will see from the ideas and inventions in this book.

We think that people should have the right to choose their own tools of self-development. In 1980, with the invention of the AEM, attempts were made to discourage and stop our work with crystals. The book *Crystal Power* is still boycotted and discriminated against by some "New Age Dealers" because it mentions and shows pictures of early AEMs, even though it doesn't tell how to build one.

Since *Crystal Power* was published in 1985, one of the most common requests is, "How can I obtain or build an AEM." By now, you may be asking, "What's an AEM?" AEM stands for autoelectromag, the most powerful of the crystal energy projectors. Work in developing the AEMs has continued steadily for ten years since the early prototypes of 1980. Newer models include more variety than those shown in *Crystal Power*, with many being smaller, lighter, and more sophisticated.

Crystal tools introduced in *Crystal Warrior* also include many post-AEM inventions spanning the decade from the eighties to the nineties. Ancient crystal weapons, crystal swords and daggers, crystal self-defense sticks, crystal container rods, and even crystal frivolities, all serve to integrate the Earth's mineral kingdom into modern society's search for spiritual development and harmony. The crystal path of the ancients can be walked in new ways; we can explore new areas together. When these new places are explored with the one inner/outer connection, a more comprehensive understanding of ourselves and our world can be reached.

To use a popular phrase, we are seeking to discover and explore new worlds within and around us. As humans, we invent and build tools to help us in our quest for knowledge, understanding, and experience. While we draw on ancient and traditional practices, the spirit of adventure leads us to create the new traditions of our changing times by daring to probe into the unknown and look at old ideas in new ways.

Self-development and exploration into new fields of life and energy can be an exciting adventure. By building and using Buck Rogers-type tools and crystal devices we can make our own inner-life explorations an adventure more mysterious and thrilling than episodes of "Star Trek" that can be watched on TV.

Due to the unusual nature of some of the inventions described in this book, the authors can't be responsible for how they are built or used. We offer you the opportunity to try these tools for yourself as a crystal warrior and offer best wishes to you on your exciting journey of self-discovery.

—*Michael G. Smith & Lin Westhorp*

Introduction

We are the creators and judges of our own reality.

In *Crystal Warrior* we will continue the adventure started in *Crystal Power* and *Crystal Spirit*, exploring the understanding and practical use of crystal energies. We'll discover that balanced energy provides the key to ourselves and our personal transformation. With the help of crystal tools, we will come to realize that we are the embodiment of Earth energy and that our understanding and use of this natural energy will lead us to happier, healthier lives.

First, we'll venture into the world of the crystal warrior, a world of balance that uses the autoelectromags combined with shamanism, the martial arts, magic, and alchemical techniques to aid in the evolution of the warrior and the Earth. These Earth-oriented practices are the keystone to the warrior's transformation. The inner evolution of these practices from ancient to modern times has remained almost invisible, like an iceberg, with only a small tip showing. Here, we'll make a larger, dynamic part of that activity visible. We'll learn of the self-control and sense of responsibility that building and using the AEMs imparts to this peaceful warrior.

The ancient alchemist sought to transmute base metals into gold and find an ultimate cure for disease that would lead to the achievement of eternal life. The modern alchemists may use either or both of these goals in the alchemical process of transforming something ordinary into something precious—themselves.

Witches and warlocks, practitioners of both ancient and modern magic, seek power and influence over natural forces by using charms, spells, magical rites and incantations. The shaman uses magic for curing disease or divining and influencing events or situations. And the martial arts practitioner seeks to gain inner peace and spiritual regeneration by the controlled use of his or her body. We'll find the thread of spirit that all these practices have in common and see how we can apply this to modern living, with the use of crystal psychotronic devices.

For the first time, crystal projectors will be introduced and their evolution from weapons to tools for spiritual development will be explored. We'll find that the alchemical process is a major factor in the construction and use of crystal devices. Many of the magical tools used in the process of self-transformation can help us extend our conscious awareness further out into the physical world. This is similar to the martial arts practice of extending the *chi* energy out beyond the body. The psychotronic AEM as a magical tool is a true energy projector, not just an extension of the physical arm and hand.

We'll meet the modern shaman, who uses psychotronic devices, crystal jewelry, and more, in new and unusual ways, adapting the practices to our fast-changing world.

Then we'll travel the Earth energy pathway through the crystal garden and on into the sanctuary of the crystal rock garden. We'll learn how to apply crystals and Earth Energy to our own personal lifestyles for better health—growing our own natural food in an environment that is beneficial to all life and transforming our drinking water for increased energy and vitality. We will also learn how to build and use aura-amplifying crystal devices to wear or carry with us for health and protection.

We'll go on to discover a personal energy shield that can be expanded into a household energy shield, programmed by ourselves to use powerful universal and Earth energies to protect home and family.

We will create the magic healing circles of old and new, using a variety of tools and natural stones for empowering our own magical world reality.

We'll learn how to build ancient crystal tools, swords and daggers along with new devices, such as the crystal self-defense sticks and explore the magical use of jewelry.

There are endless varieties of tools and devices that can be constructed using crystals. Both ordinary and unusual crystal devices are introduced here for the first time. We urge you to look at some of our favorites included in the Appendix, along with instructions for making them. It would be a shame if you missed out on the new rods for the 1990s, including the beautiful wooden rod (our all-time favorite), the unusual spike rod, practical container rod, expanding extension rod and powerful squeeze-light rods. In the second section of the Appendix, are the charged piezo rods and some lighthearted adaptations of everyday objects into crystal devices.

After reading *Crystal Power* and *Crystal Spirit* many people have written to say they were designing and building their own crystal inventions. We hope *Crystal Warrior*, along with the ideas and inventions included here will inspire you to continue to find new and creative ways to use the crystals that are so willing to help us develop our human potential to create a better world for us all.

This wide-ranging, comprehensive overview of human action and experience should provide you with something you can use in your own personal practice of the art of life. We hope you enjoy the adventurous path of the crystal warrior, which leads from ourselves to the Earth and back again with a whole new attitude for living healthy, powerful and balanced lives.

ENERGY MAGIC FOR TODAY

Traditional Earth people have always quietly gone about their business, adapting and using whatever is practical from the society and time they happen to be living in. Some ideas from the past are kept and some are discarded in favor of ones more in tune with the times. Earth energy workers and their craft are always growing and changing in their personal relationship to the Earth. These practitioners realize that part of life and growth is change and they modify their practices as they, too, grow and change, creating new forms of energy with each new day. They don't hesitate to take, use and adapt anything available that might be of practical use in working the magic of inner and outer transformation.

For the Native American shaman, buckskins, buffalo robes, and moccasins have been replaced by blue jeans, ski jackets, and boots or tennis shoes. Horses have been replaced by cars and pickup trucks. And tepees and caves have evolved into houses and trailers. The practical Earth people of today, who are more interested in results than in form, are always adapting and changing with the times. They bring about a new synthesis of the old Earth magic with changing conditions whenever possible.

Since Earth-oriented spiritual practices have been kept private for so long, it's difficult to estimate the number of practitioners in the world today. A fair guess would be in the hundreds of millions. With this many workers, Earth-oriented prayers and ceremonies are having a beneficial healing effect on the Earth. Prayers and healing circles during full moons, solstices and equinoxes have beneficial effects on the people who do them, all other life forms, and the Earth herself. This is so, regardless of whether the point of view of the practitioner is shamanistic, Wicca, magical, martial arts, new age, or any combination of these. The common key is the Earth orientation. This common denominator ties the various practices together. The new religions such as Judaism, Islam and Christianity are much poorer for lack of an Earth orientation that leads to a reverence and respect for all life, of which humanity is only a small part.

In all religions, however, there can be a tendency to forget the universal balance of male and female. For example, in Native American shamanism, it is commonly accepted to think of the Earth Mother and the Sky Father. In reality, our universe is a balance of polarity. Humans, regardless of their sex, are a balance of both female and male energies. There is a balance of positive and negative, male and female inherent in everything. This means that, in order to get in tune with the Universal Law of Balance, we should not forget that the Earth Mother also embodies an Earth Father and the Sky Father embodies a Sky Mother. This balance of energy exists and flows through all things in our world. Disharmony occurs when humans block or refuse to acknowledge these energies. This reflects in our inner selves, and more dramatically, in our outer world, situations, and events.

In many Earth oriented practices, acknowledgment is given to the powers and winds: east, south, west, north, up (to the Sky Father), and down (to the Earth Mother), making six directions in all. An appropriate way to expand this with our new awareness and understanding would be to acknowledge both the Sky Father and Sky Mother upwards and the Earth Mother and Earth Father downwards. This is more in harmony with the universe and the Earth. Old traditions change, grow and evolve in this way into new traditions of the time and space we are living in.

This acknowledgment of the male and female balance can be applied to Native American pipe ceremonies, magical Earth circles and all other spiritual or self-developmental practices. The benefits of practicing with balanced energy are as unlimited as the universe itself. The connection of an individual to the universe and attunement to the Earth can best be harmoniously achieved by realization of the male and female principle joined within and without ourselves and all of creation.

Male and female balance is especially reflected in nurturing and caring for plants and gardens. The magical garden is a natural ecosystem that allows male and female, positive and negative, a chance to find their own perfect balance. The seasons of the Earth along with the life cycles of growing plants and the cycles of the moon represent the basis of magical Earth practices that tune in to and use this balance. Earth magic and healing circles are not just a carry-over from the past. Earth-oriented healing circles are even more important now, with our present environmental concerns, than they ever were in the past. Most religions are finally realizing that environmental care is a relevant part of religious practice.

Personal spiritual growth and balance has always been part of religious practice. The key point to remember is that growth needs a healthy environment to take place in, making the growing movement for a clean Earth necessary for human development and conscious awareness.

The Earth is Mother and Father to all human life. Spirit beings of light we may be, but on Earth we have chosen to demonstrate our spirits within physical bodies that need to be cared for. Our bodies are formed from the materials of the Earth and are nurtured by water and food from living plants and animals. This cycle of life is an interdependent self-generating process which shows that humans and Earth are one with life, not separate. This is the basic understanding and realization of magical Earth religions and martial arts, both ancient and modern. Magical balance easily equates to ecological balance. Ecological balance of the environment will bring back the natural harmony of the Earth magic that was taken for granted by the ancients.

Ceremonial healing circles, sending the energy of love to the Earth, need to be augmented by recycling efforts, planting trees and gardens, along with practical actions of cleaning up the land, air and water in our environment. All are equally important to ourselves and the Earth. Driving less, or driving more fuel-efficient cars with emission controls, may not seem like a romantic magical process, but when we think about the benefits we derive from helping to promote an ecology that is balanced with modern technology we can see that it is pretty magical. Most ancient magicians would trade their staffs and swords for an automobile (the magic chariot) or color television (the all-seeing eye that enables us to view events all over the world).

Ancient magic was a way to make life easier and to gain a higher standard of living, health and whatever other benefits could be derived from it: good hunting and abundant crops, etc. Most of the things we take for granted today would be considered high magic by the practitioners of old. Lighted and heated homes, with radios, VCRs, stereos, telephones, carpeting, hot and cold running water, would have been considered almost the ultimate magic.

Modern health care, medicine and stores with an abundance of food would seem like a wondrous miracle to the high priests of the ancients. Air travel with modern planes and helicopters would have been seen as travel for the gods.

We've seen what we have that the ancients lacked, but what did they have that draws us to a study of those religions? What is it that we seek through the practice of Earth magic or martial arts? They didn't have the modern magic of technology, but the ancient practices did bring a sense of inner peace and oneness with the Earth. It also brought about a feeling of personal power, self-confidence and self-respect. These are qualities, lacking in much of our modern society, that we need to regain.

Inner self-transformation is where the Earth religions, magic and martial arts evolve into alchemy. The practitioners become something other than what they started out as—more aware and in balance with the Earth, the universe and themselves.

Shamanic transformation is an expansion of the alchemical process to unite the inner balance of the individual with the outer balance of the Earth. Earth energies, by nature, are a balance of male and female energies. Nature always seeks a balance. It is only human beings who are sometimes unaware or unconscious of their balance of energy. In humans, those who are consciously aware, seek this balance by choice and understanding. Attunement with the Earth energies through shamanic practices is one of the most natural ways of growing into the balance of self, Earth and universal. Most ancient peoples and societies were aware of this need. They geared their religions and customs toward seeking this balance. Modern-day people are only now becoming more and more aware of this natural inner need because we are suffering from a lack of balanced energies.

The shamanic pipe ceremony and the magic circle of the sword or dagger align us with the natural energy forces of the Earth and attune our consciousness to the planetary consciousness. We are one and the same at this point. Our will for healing balance is always accepted by the Earth and reflected in outward manifestations that are beneficial to all.

PART I

SHAMAN AND WARRIOR

The shaman/warrior is a balanced blend of feminine and masculine energies. Attunement to the planetary consciousness through magical ritual and healing ceremonies channel the energy of the Earth Mother/Father. Likewise, the practices of the Earth religions channel the energies of the Sky Father/Mother. We live in a universe where the balance of polarities—positive and negative, black and white, male and female—is necessary for inner and outer harmony.

When this state of awareness is attained, we flow easily into the stream of conscious energy. The warrior or shaman becomes a clear channel for directing energy to where it can bring about the healing of ourselves, our planet and the Earth's inhabitants. Achieving this is merely a matter of unblocking the natural flow of energy in ourselves by becoming aware of it. Crystal projectors can be the key that starts this unblocking process.

Once we realize that we each create our own reality on a personal level, and the blend of our minds creates the world's reality, we step into a position of power where we can change and modify that reality if we choose. Building and using a variety of crystal tools will help us in this. Personal reality changes for the better and faster when the mind, body, heart and spirit are augmented by crystal tools that amplify what we are, as well as what we desire, while tuning us to a higher level of vibrations.

In this section we'll explore what it's like to be a modern shaman who blends old traditions with new practices to fit the world of today. Then we'll take a look at the crystal warrior. What motivates him or her? What is the warrior trying to achieve as a spiritual being? What is the role of weapons in the crystal warrior's development? We'll find that the real battle of the crystal warrior is an inner one that allows control over self and environment.

The last three chapters are devoted to the autoelectromags. These projectors combine black box psionics with the use of crystals to further our ability to create a better reality. The evolvement and workings of the autoelectromags are explored and detailed instructions are given for building and using these tools.

The autoelectromag may be the weapon of the future that shapes our world into one of peace and spiritual harmony. Once we realize that our enemies are merely the reflections of our own disordered thoughts, it will be possible to love these reflections of ourselves and live in harmony with them. When we've accomplished this, we can progress to higher level spiritual challenges that preclude war and strife. Only then, will we realize our full potential as Children of the Light.

Chapter 1

THE MODERN SHAMAN

The vehicle of the shaman is frequently a car.

The modern shaman usually has one very traditional characteristic. That is, the use or adaptation of anything that will help achieve the shaman's goals. A good example of this is the automobile. Few Native American shamans travel by horseback or walk hundreds of miles these days. A shaman without a modern means of transportation would be very limited and ineffective. Most modern shamans are also urban or suburban shamans who have to drive to work each day.

Being a modern practitioner of the arts is not just something done at home anymore. The shaman of today usually has various crystals, rocks, wooden artifacts and other devices that travel with him in his car or truck. Sometimes crystal and rock arrangements are placed on the console of today's iron horse. It's not unusual to see a crystal pendulum hanging from the rearview mirror of the shaman's vehicle. Psychotronic devices, like crystal rods, pipes and AEMs are frequently carried in automobiles.

Shamanism is a spiritualizing process that goes on all the time, not just during a healing circle or prayer ceremony for a full moon, solstice or equinox. Shamanism in modern times goes much further then just working Earth magic at certain prescribed times and places. It's a state of being, combined with a process of doing, and it goes on all the time. Growth of conscious awareness and attunement to the planetary consciousness is a twenty-four hour a day process of self-transformation. This ongoing process can be augmented with ceremonies and gatherings with other like-minded people, but the inner individual is always the key component.

Sometimes, as an aid to the shamanic process, jewelry is worn. Native American shamans are often partial to silver and turquoise jewelry. Medicine bags can contain stones that are meaningful to the shaman, and crystals are used during ceremonies. A primitive medicine necklace with a variety of stones and trinkets radiates the healing energy of the Earth during a prayer ceremony with a sacred pipe. During a healing circle, the touch of hands with a person wearing their favorite ring boosts the energy of the whole circle. Gemstones on anklets balance the flow and movement of dancers in certain ceremonies.

The modern shaman also uses a variety of psychotronic devices. Psychotronic tools can cover a wide range, in a variety of forms. The crystal rod, staff, dagger and sword are among the most common in use. Various drums, rattles and pipes (including the crystal medicine pipe described in *Crystal Spirit*) are also popular for the new shaman.

The newest tool of the shaman is the psychotronic autoelectromag projector, or AEM. The AEM is the first really different magical tool to arise in thousands of years. The wand, staff, sword and dagger extend the energy of the practitioner. The AEM, however, is the first psychotronic tool to allow a more intense projection of that energy. It combines the unlimited potential of the human spirit with psychotronic power. A projection of energy, guided by carrier waves of human thought and emotion, can be sent like a laser. This laser-like beam is the difference between the extensions of the sword or wand and the autoelectromag.

Magical tools are often weapons. A fascination with weapons is something that has prevailed throughout history. Weapons represent personal power, security and safety through self-protection. Magical weapons are tools for increasing our personal power and spiritual growth.

When a weapon comes into magical use, it gives us the power to change and transform our lives for the better. The magical weapon becomes a tool for acquiring self-control, and allows the practitioner to bring about a personal transformation. The weapon is also a tool for acquiring knowledge and growth that brings about self-transformation.

THE MAGIC CIRCLE

One of the most often used symbols of the shaman, no matter what tools, implements or devices are used, is the circle. Rocks, stones and crystals are frequently used to mark the directions of the circle. A large area is not needed to create a magic circle. The setting of rocks and crystals in an area of just a couple of feet is all that is necessary for creating the center of a circle that can be expanded to any size the shaman desires.

The following diagrams show a few examples of the arrangements of the center of a shamanic circle using only a foot or two of space. Many combinations are possible for center circle arrangements. The important thing is to make one using your favorite rocks and crystals. (For more information about the actual process of the pipe ceremony or the healing circle see Chapter 15.)

In later years the environment has been a major concern of the modern shaman. Environmental healing of the Earth is needed on such a wide scale that regular healing ceremonies need to be augmented by unusual means.

Shamanistic, as well as magical and alchemical processes, can be applied to healing the Earth's environment. A single prayer by one person can reach out through the Earth's energy network to produce a positive influence. A shamanic healing circle created by one or more people can amplify thoughts, emotions and psychic energy to act like a high voltage generator that sends waves of healing energy in all directions across the Earth's gridwork-pattern energy field. The web of life connects everything on Earth, but is not used by everyone to promote beneficial healing and balance. The shaman who is aware of this energy network can effect powerful energy changes anywhere on Earth with a simple circle ceremony.

ROCK HEALING CIRCLES

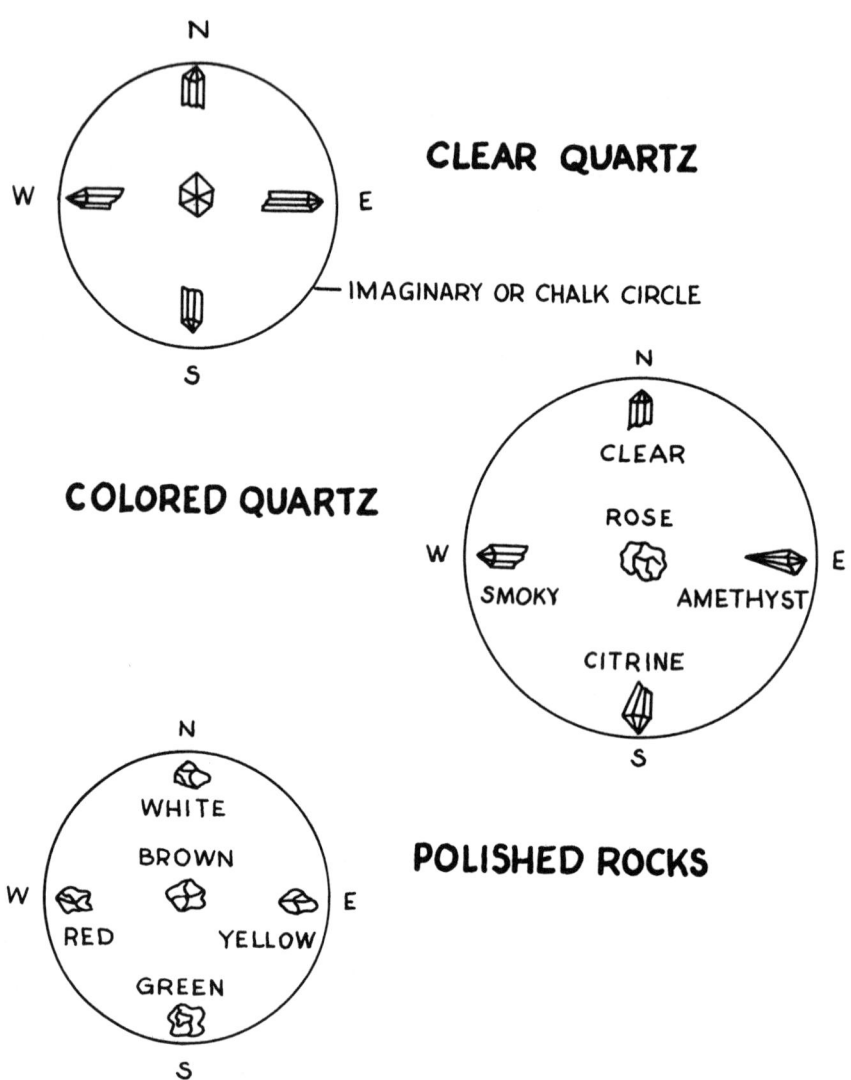

Chapter 2

THE CRYSTAL WARRIOR

We, of the Earth, make up the One that is the Universe.

The crystal warrior is motivated by love and a sense of connection to everything in the universe. He or she knows that life involves the interaction of life forms, and that out of these interactions come growth and the experience of oneness. The belief that it is not enough to just "do no harm," but that "good" can be done while "doing no harm" is inherent to this path.

The crystal warrior knows that love can be actively expressed even when meeting the parts of ourselves that are "so-called" enemies. When we are told to love our enemies, it is because they are reflections of ourselves. Loving an enemy can be difficult, but has been proven possible by people who have made a conscious effort towards growth. The warrior seeks to make this possibility a reality in all meetings with other beings, knowing that he and his enemy are sharing an experience that can help both of them grow.

The crystal warrior utilizes the conscious expansion of the aura of *ki* or *chi* life energy. This expansion of energy, with practice, can be enlarged into a sphere that encompasses the Earth, the universe, and all its many dimensions. The basic tools are the crystal warrior himself/herself, and the crystal or crystal tool used in harmony with the warrior's sphere of life energy.

The process is alchemical in nature, transforming the warrior during the use of crystal tools, or, more often, during the building and construction of crystal tools. Our oneness with all of creation means that we are also one with the Universal Life Energy. The process of creating and using crystal tools helps us learn how to use this energy in the never-ending expansion of human consciousness, growth and creation.

Spiritual warriors of many ages have followed this path, frequently opening new frontiers of human experience. The development of Zen archery was a major new form of spiritual practice at one time. In Zen archery the arrow is assumed to be already at the target. There's no need for tension, striving or apprehension for the archer. It is already done so the archer can be calm, relaxed and peaceful. This principle can be applied to the use of all tools of spiritual development: swords, staffs, knives, wands, projectors, etc.

Miyamoto Musashi, author of *The Strategy of Five Rings*, changed from the metal sword to the wooden sword, or *bokkan*, which in his hands was just as effective. Today, many types of *bokkans* and wooden swords are used in various forms of the martial arts. The practice of these arts can be deadly when used for offense or defense, yet their true value shines through as a tool of individual understanding and spiritual development.

The path of the warrior in other societies has led to the use of metal swords and daggers as tools of the magical alchemical process. In secret societies across the Earth, the warrior became the healer, magician and medicine man. This evolved by using swords and daggers for magical spiritual practices. Individuals in secret groups used these tools in sacred circles with practices that brought about the magical alchemy of spiritual growth and inner transformation.

For example, a sword was used to point to each of the four directions during a circle of prayers and chants. Then the energy of Earth, Air, Fire and Water was called upon. In this manner the weapon used transformed the practitioner by a magical alchemy into a spiritual warrior.

The use of swords and daggers throughout the ages has brought an understanding of the spiritual forces of creation and the individual knowledge of oneness that cannot be taught in words, but can be experienced directly by the individual.

This type of warrior path has also been the way of some Native Americans. The war drums, war chants, war dance, and the tomahawk pipe were transformed into the stone pipe of peace, and later, to the crystal pipe of universal understanding and unconditional love. (For more information on the crystal pipe read *Crystal Spirit*.) Drums, dances and channeled chants are now being used with crystal pipes to reach out to the Universal Sky Father/Mother and send out the circle of healing energy to the Earth Mother/Father and her people.

What began, over and over again, as weapons of war and strife, have progressed on the path of the warrior to spiritual tools of growth, understanding—and peace. The bamboo wands and the crystal pointed staff in the hands of the physical warrior became tools of change and transformation to the spiritual warrior.

No matter which direction the warrior turns, he or she is always connected to the *ki*, or life, energy. This energy expands outward as it is externalized, manifesting as a sphere in the outer world. The sphere may be slightly oval, like the aura of a plant, animal or human, and is a three-dimensional energy form that is living, breathing and alive.

The inner world of the warrior could be described as a circle or a spiral. The crystal warrior is most likely to be one with this moving path when he or she is constructing or using a crystal tool. The path then becomes spiraling energy moving within a pulsating sphere, expanding and contracting with each breath. The warrior who has experienced his oneness with the universe will know the right time to do "something" and the right time to do "nothing." He or she can be transformed by doing something, but can be equally transformed by doing nothing.

This is the world of soul, spirit, heart and the energy of unconditional love in creation. We all have access to it.

Can the path of the crystal warrior work in modern society? Whatever ideas one might have about the way of the warrior, it is a way that can be tested and developed further in our modern times than it could have been in any historical era.

The meaning of life, as an opportunity to meet and communicate with other beings for the experience of growth, can be stimulated by today's lifestyles. There is more knowledge and more opportunity for growth available on Earth now than at any other time in recorded history.

The path of the crystal warrior opens doorways to a large number of growth experiences using the key of the crystal. This path is not for squeamish dabblers. Many of our most important growth experiences might not be considered "good" if hastily judged. Losing a loved one, job or home may seem like a great tragedy when it happens; but often that loss will lead the warrior to take the next step in growth that leads to a fuller, richer life than would otherwise have been possible.

Many who are on the path to enlightenment think that we are being assaulted by the media with negative programming in the form of movies, radio, television and advertising, as well as the tragedies on the nightly news. The crystal warrior sees all these so-called assaults as ways to learn about different people, places and conditions, providing more life experiences for growth when viewed through the eyes of wisdom. We can travel the world and see more people, places and things through the media than we could ever do in person in a lifetime. Why not take advantage of this abundance of information and experience? Nature, travel and people shows can be used to learn and grow with an expanded perception of our world and all its creations.

Many city dwellers don't get out to the country, mountains, or seashore as often as they wish. A television program about animals, birds, flowers, rocks or undersea life can be a refreshing change of pace that is easily accessible to all of us.

Some people think that our modern cities with people packed together are a disadvantage. Cities do, however, allow us the advantage of meeting more people and personality types than we have in many lifetimes so that we can have more growth experiences.

A life-growth experience in the city can be as quick as observing someone during the rush hour traffic or as complex as meeting and interacting with forty new people face-to-face during a seminar or workshop.

All situations hold growth potential for the crystal warrior, even when he or she isn't actively working with crystals. The simple act of putting seed in a bird feeder and meeting a squirrel and eight small birds can bring enlightenment to the warrior. The same can be said for planting the garden or mowing the lawn, since during these activities, one who is aware can meet many beings from the various life kingdoms of the Earth. The robin, the earthworm, the grasshopper, all are beings that can help us grow by observing them. It's not just the raven, the bear, the eagle or the elk who are important to meet. All of the Earth's inhabitants are important, even the smallest sparrow or earthworm.

The same philosophy holds true for people. It's exciting to meet the famous musician at a concert or the well-known politician or author at a dinner banquet. These can be meetings in life for growth. Yet, there is much more on the path of the warrior. Many times it's just as important to meet the retired couple at a garage sale or the young student at the library. The meeting doesn't even have to be direct to stimulate growth. It can be the old man ahead of you in a check-out line, sharing a life experience with the checker, that provides the clue to something that's been troubling you. The warrior is aware or becomes more aware of the subtlest meanings of senses and perceptions. Warriors are not so caught up in their own world of thoughts that they fail to notice the finer shades of the colors of life around them.

The unconditional love energy of the One World of Spirit is unlimited for the crystal warrior who is sensitive and attuned to that universal world. Opportunities for the crystal warrior's growth are endless with the use of that love energy.

Chapter 3

THE CRYSTAL WARRIOR'S WEAPONS

*There are times, in our society,
when we must resort to thinking.*

The crystal warrior, in essence, is weaponless since the warrior does not see a hostile world and the possibility of meeting an enemy. What other people perceive as weapons—a crystal knife, crystal sword or crystal projector—the warrior sees as tools for meeting with and exploring other aspects of self.

The warrior is aware of energy fields and fluctuations in these fields. In most situations, the warrior senses disturbed or unbalanced energy fields, where a confrontation might be developing, and simply arranges not to be there. The condition for a battle requires two sides for conflict. When one side or one combatant doesn't show up, there's no fight or war, only peace.

Some Native American tribes used this strategy. They were aware, through keen senses, of where the U.S. cavalry was at any given time and avoided being there. Conscious awareness and a trust of one's inner promptings is necessary to use this strategy successfully and consistently.

What of the rare instance when one is there? It sometimes happens. When it does, the warrior's motivation of love and sense of oneness come into play. The crystal warrior sees another aspect of self that must be neutralized or disarmed without harming the other aspect. To harm another is to harm ourselves, and conversely, what we are one with cannot harm us. This is easier said than done. In the heat of the moment, facing an armed assailant, it's easy to forget that the assailant and the gun are other aspects of ourselves.

This is why spiritual practice with crystal tools is important. The use of these tools can lead to an understanding, through experience, that we are all connected by the life energy. There is no substitute for the conscious awareness of oneness. Words, books and philosophers can't replace the experience of being at one with self.

Being at one is being in balance. Confrontations, fights and wars can only occur when two sides, or two people, who are out of balance meet. If one side or one person realizes this and consciously regains balance, harmony and peace are restored. Maintaining balance within, the crystal warrior does not go to war and the war does not come to the warrior.

The Earth Mother doesn't fight herself. The universe doesn't battle with itself. The life energy, all of creation's energy, flows and grows. Nature is our great teacher. The energy of nature is everywhere. We don't have to go to a forty dollar lecture or a five hundred dollar seminar to learn. Our teachers are always around and within us. We don't have to wait for an expert or a messiah. Our Great Teacher is already here, within, and always has been. We don't have to go anywhere. The *ki*, the *chi*, the force is always available to us. Through conscious awareness and being in balance, we go with the natural flow of energy that takes us to many wondrous places on the path of life. The crystal warrior goes with the energy, but knows he can't go anywhere to get the energy since it's already there.

The old saying of, "What we think it is—it isn't, and what we think it isn't—it is," still holds true in modern times. It's the difference between "flowing like water" and "throwing stones at the wind."

The flow of this invisible, undefinable, energy is always with us. The degree or strength of the flow is the changing part of the unchanging energy. The flow in a person can range from barely being alive to being creative, powerful, and dynamic. This is a very wide range and the balanced, high-energy side is definitely more fun as a growing experience.

Being in balance with this flow also affects the aura. Of course a balanced healthy aura of bright energy feels better, but the field of this aura in the universal flow can vary a great deal, even in balance. The field of the aura can be a few feet, half a mile, or unlimited.

Experience with the energy, using meditation, martial arts or crystal tools, can expand and extend the energy range of the crystal warrior's aura. Prayer, pipe ceremonies, healing circles and spiritual practices can also expand this field of energy. Not every practice is right for everybody. We need to experiment to find out what works best for us. Even this can change in time. Being aware and changing patterns or practices is often needed in the course of a lifetime. We can no longer afford to be afraid to change.

Chapter 4

THE INNER BATTLE

A New Age in finite. We live to create a new world that is infinite—always in the act of creation.

The conflict or battle of the spiritual crystal warrior is the inner battle with various aspects of self. When a person is on the path of the crystal warrior, all battles are within, on a mental, emotional or spiritual plane.

Most illnesses and symptoms relating to health are a result of inner conflict. The inner conflict must be resolved to a state of balance in order to promote good health. Strangely enough, good health is not the main goal. Health is a side effect of good life, good living and peaceful thoughts. Being happily in balance with ourselves is the key.

The reflection of the same balance or lack of it in our world society is expressed in our environment. The Earth's environment reflects the balance of society or mass consciousness the same way the body and health reflect the balance of the individual. Our inner thoughts, on both a personal and global level, and what we see and experience around us are directly correlated.

Being a crystal warrior is an art, not just related to martial arts, but all arts. The crystal warrior becomes more in tune and in balance with the creative energy of the universe and the earth as he or she evolves. The natural flow of this energy becomes the expression of creativity in many areas of life.

This expression comes out in many forms, frequently simultaneously. The warrior finds himself or herself becoming, not just the martial artist or inventor of new forms of crystal tools and devices, but also becoming the musician, writer, sculptor, artist, singer, dancer, actor/actress, comedian, architect, builder, landscaper, gardener . . . and even more in experiencing new forms and practices of creativity. The energy flows to and through the crystal warrior so it must come out and show up somewhere.

The invisible energy of non-being becomes the visible form and practice of life as art. This is not so much something crystal warriors try to do as it is something that happens spontaneously, many times without thought or logical planning. It comes from growth and just being. The energy of love through the crystal warrior expresses itself as the creation of art.

The warrior follows the path of soul growth and evolvement no matter where it leads. Anyone who follows this path expresses or manifests through creation. Some of the most enjoyable creations are music, song, dance and art. Many crystal warriors either are or become singers, dancers, musicians, song writers, artists or artisans. Artistry and healing are expressions of the crystal warrior's path. Life itself becomes an art at one point along the universal trail. Balanced creativity expresses itself in harmony with the nature of the chosen course. When the warrior makes the conscious choice to be attuned with the Earth and the universe, growth and creation become the main reason for living. This comes about naturally by understanding and accepting self with unconditional love.

Chapter 5

AUTOELECTROMAG (AEM)

The New Age movement is a survival movement, with instinct and love creating a "New World."

WHAT IS THE AUTOELECTROMAG OR AEM?

The autoelectromag (AEM) is a special type of projector used for spiritual development. It isn't a firearm, projectile weapon, or a laser. Instead, it's a psionic beam generator in the form of a hand-held projector—the synthesis of the early radionic machines or black boxes, with their simple electronic circuitry, and the quartz crystal power rods of the ancients.

The electronics of the projector are simple, using an insulated copper chamber, wiring, and a quartz crystal, through which a beam, created and controlled by the mind and thoughts of the operator, is focused. Its workings are similar to electricity in the sense that to wire an electric light and flip the switch to turn it on, no vast knowledge of electrical theory is necessary. The results are obtained by simple procedures, whether the entire theory is understood or not.

The AEM was first invented in 1980. It was an over-sized heavy projector with a shape similar to many science fiction-type blasters popularized in the movies and in adventure novels. The second prototype created was a longer version of the original AEM, in the form of a rifle, with a shoulder stock and telescopic sight. The third generation of the subatomic projector, created in 1982, was a scaled-down version of the original AEM, roughly about eight inches long, in the form of a small pocket projector. Regardless of their shapes or sizes, these thought/energy projectors all work in the same manner.

THE PRINCIPLE BEHIND THE AEM

It has become increasingly obvious through scientific discoveries that we exist as part of one large field of energy. This field can be perceived as a vast sea of particles, waves and interacting fields.

To see how these fields work, let's look at a grain of sand. This piece of material is radiating an electrodynamic energy field, small but nonetheless there. The same applies to a larger mineral, such as a rock or a rock crystal. Every piece of matter, whether organic or inorganic, is held together in a densely packed field and is radiating energy, or what we call an aura, from its inner structure.

We normally think of this aura as applying to humans, animals and plants, but any structure in any form has it's own energy field. These radiating fields, or auras, are interactive and connected with an overall energy field which is as large as our universe. Everything in existence is connected with all other parts of existence through this overall energy field. In the case of human beings, the thoughts from our minds create particles or waves of energy that travel virtually instantaneously. The human mind, with its thought-energy manifesting as particles, waves, or radiating fields, has a capacity to reach out and affect any other object through the already-established connections of the larger energy field.

In recent years, man invented machines of various types that amplify thought and emotional energies. This enables individuals to reach out and effect changes in the interacting fields at great distances. It is believed that emotional energy or desire acts as a carrier wave for the thought energy and creates a stronger manifestation.

The psionic projector, or AEM, uses the universal energy of the overall energy field with the added impetus of thought and emotional energy. Energy is projected by the visualization and emotional feelings of the operators. The limits of this type of operation are the same as those of human consciousness and the universe, both of which may be considered limitless. Use of this type of device on a planetary level is bound to have far-reaching effects.

Many philosophies have stated that we are one with the rest of creation. An understanding of the overall energy field supports those philosophies. By using the medium of this field we gain the ability to reach out and heal imbalances wherever we find them.

The invention of the early radionic machines, which amplified thoughts and emotions, have had a far-reaching effect in the last half of this century. The introduction of energy equipment in the 1970s that amplifies and focuses the human mind and emotions using quartz crystals has further speeded up progress in this area. In the 1980s we increased our knowledge and technical ability to amplify, project and change the different patterns in the overall energy field. One of the most significant advances in this powerful knowledge has come with the invention of the psionic beam projectors, or AEMs.

All these inventions have now been brought into use in the private or public sector of many nations on this planet. The fact that they are being used by so many people in a number of countries may be partially responsible for the significant changes that have taken place in the structure of our societies. These changes are affecting all aspects of our lives on an individual and international level, promoting more equality, and balance. Another effect has been that things that were once hidden are now out in the open. Deceit is no longer an effective tool for controlling others or hiding from oneself. This has been the most positive sign to date that a change is really taking place. Once we know the truth, we can acknowledge it, accept responsibility for our contribution to it, and change our attitudes to create a better truth.

There is probably no completely accurate way to predict the effects of the influence of radionic crystal projectors on the overall energy fields. But, because of the level of development needed to operate them, their use should have a beneficial effect on our total ecosystem. These devices promote individual responsibility and growth, and provide a new step on the frontier of evolution.

The universal knowledge of directed mind energy is being acquired by more and more people who are searching for understanding. The knowledge of how to build and develop our minds to operate powerful, far-reaching devices adds a new dimension to human experience. It's timely that these devices have appeared just when humankind has been pushed to a point of survival. Faced with the monumental challenge of healing ourselves and our world, we have to change and grow or lose the battle of evolution.

Anyone can acquire an understanding of the energies involved and build a simple low-cost device, such as the AEM, which is a powerful tool that can be used in a positive fashion to promote change. By exercising the self-control and understanding it takes to effectively use the AEMs, we acquire the power and vision to change, create and recreate the world around us. It's already happening as we become more consciously aware of ourselves and our interrelationship to other forms of energy.

There are numerous opinions and recommendations about how we, as individuals and groups, should handle our fast-changing times. We have no previous experience or guidebook to use, but crystals, psionics and the AEMs will help give us the maturity and wisdom to follow our own inner guidance to the right paths.

If we formulate a philosophy, science, or social structure today, it must, by nature, be a living, changing creation in order to attune itself with the forces that are moving in our world. There is no stable dogmatic plan of action from religion, politics, or economics that can keep up with the world we live in. As soon as something is set down as dogma, it becomes obsolete and ineffective in dealing with the current interrelationships of human beings.

This is a time of increasingly powerful energies and fast-moving events, whether in the micro-universe of the particle world, the international events of the macro-world, or in the world of interaction between galaxies of our universe. The fact that we are learning to deal with this energy indicates that we now have the opportunity to attain harmony with the universe through change.

Although peace and love have been expressed as a goal of many of our world religions, the fact that they solidified without promoting this understanding doesn't mean that it won't come about. The nature of events taking place now will continue to force us to grow and understand simply because we have to in order to save ourselves.

In the past, it's been questioned whether large numbers of people can understand and deal responsibly with the basic knowledge of how we ourselves and our world work. Our language is so limited as to make communication of this process difficult. We're communicating on an intellectual level knowledge that can be perceived only by a balance between emotional intuition and intellectual mental perception. Even with the difficulties of communication, though, we believe that a majority of people are fully capable of understanding their relationship to the world and evolving through spiritual growth. It's not a big mystery that requires secret knowledge from a religious priesthood or the obscure language of any scientific priesthood, but rather, a few simple concepts that require the intuitive understanding we're born with in order to master.

The most difficult aspect of this communication comes from the fact that it has not been done before on a wide scale. We are at a place in development that we simply have not been at before. This is part of the struggle and challenge of growing.

THE AEM AS A TOOL OF CHANGE

Many weapons of the past have been turned into tools of spiritual development. A good example of this is the bow and arrow used in Zen archery, where the arrow is already at the target in the mind of the archer before he notches his arrow. No worry or effort is required in shooting the arrow because the archer is one with bow, arrow and target.

The same attitude of spirit can be applied to the crystal sword and the AEM. Practice with these devices can be carried out with complete calm and relaxation. No striving effort is necessary. The deed is already done by virtue of the practitioner being one with all of creation.

TURNING GUNS INTO SPIRITUAL PROJECTORS

Staffs and swords (usually wooden or bamboo) are also used in some types of martial arts practice. These are just a few of the many weapons now used as tools of spiritual, mental and physical development. Since these weapons are used in such a wide variety of techniques, styles and form, why not use guns as well? If ancient weapons can be applied to inner growth and development, so can modern weapons evolve into personal tools of creative awareness.

Guns are prevalent in most countries and societies on Earth. They are now an integral part of our world society as tools and symbols of personal power. Guns are a creation of ours that need to be faced and understood.

When a weapon is perceived as a weapon, it reflects a consciousness that hasn't developed its full powerful potential. However, when a sword, knife, or gun is seen as a tool for self-development, the process of individual conscious growth is in action.

Guns in our society, for the most part, have been a reflection of fear, insecurity, powerlessness, and alienation. Take, for example, the practice of hunting for sport, killing our brothers and sisters—animals, birds and creatures of the sea—for nothing more than pleasure. We often use the excuse that it's our instinct for survival that causes us to kill, but it isn't true. Sport hunting is a poor substitute for taking individual responsibility for understanding oneself and then using that understanding to benefit life rather than kill it.

There should be laws to protect the rights and lives of animals as well as people. This would help during our transition into an evolved society. Recognition in public and in our laws of animals' rights would also have an effect on mass consciousness that would help bring about the understanding that all creatures are spiritual beings that deserve the consideration we give ourselves.

The primary effect on mass consciousness will still come from changing our perception of guns, from weapons, to projectors, or tools of personal and spiritual development. This could be especially helpful with the younger, TV and video game generation, whose views will certainly help create the world of the future. A child who sees people casually killing each other with weapons on TV will imitate the mentality that teaches life is cheap, even if he never actually picks up a gun and shoots someone. The child that sees weapons being used for spiritual development that enhances a reverence for life, will also imitate that attitude.

Guns have traditionally been used as a substitute for and a way to avoid self-development and personal responsibility. The new trend is to use them for just the opposite—personal growth and expansion.

Guns as tools for personal development, used with martial arts practices, can have a widespread appeal to all generations. The history of humankind is a history of violence and weapons, even in modern times. Yet, any time a common weapon was used as a self-development tool, miraculous changes came about, as we have seen by the use of martial arts for personal development rather than to promote violence.

Efficiency and accuracy in using various tools has inevitably progressed to incredible achievements in personal growth and awareness. It's worked successfully with every tool humans have ever invented, as well as the human body itself. Efficiency with any tool is one vehicle for achieving balance and harmony with the mind, body and spirit so that they become one with the Source or Universal Mind. Relaxation and natural movements, like a dance, lead to personal harmony that radiates outward to affect the overall energy field of mass consciousness that, minute by minute, creates the world around us.

USING THE AUTOELECTROMAGS

It's interesting that the pattern of the construction of psionic or psychotronic devices is more important than the parts themselves. The important thing is that the pattern be complete and all the contacts solid so the overall pattern is connected. A greater understanding of these peculiar characteristics can be achieved through the study of psionics, sometimes called psychotronics.

There are two methods of using the AEM projectors. The first uses a photograph or television picture of the target, whether a machine, a human being, or an area of the Earth's surface. Focus the picture in your mind while focusing the projector on the target. Then hold down the momentary contact switch while visualizing the particle beam projecting from the crystal tip to the target. This projection can be imagined as entering the television screen and following the UHF carrier waves to a satellite and back down to the source. Or, it can be visualized as entering the picture and following a path across the Earth's magnetic (geomagnetic) field lines of force about five feet above the ground, then reaching a target as far away as the other side of the Earth. The beam can also be imagined as emitting particles that disappear in the immediate area of the operator and reappear at any distance you wish, before entering the target. The particles travel virtually instantaneously.

In the old days, photographs for which the negative had not been destroyed were sometimes inserted into the early black box-type machines. This is not the case with the AEMs. The picture to be focused on is set in front of the operator or can be one on the TV screen.

In the second method of operation, the picture of the target is merely visualized in the mind, without the aid of a photograph or television image. The AEM is then aimed with the switch depressed and the projection of the AEM's beam follows the previous pattern of imagining the particle beam following the lines of the Earth's magnetic field to the target, or disappearing in the operator's area and reappearing near the target.

The processes for both methods of operation are the same in effect, but it requires more practice to use visualization without a photograph.

Another facet of operation is the emotional desire of the operator of the projector. An emotional desire increases the intensity of the projected beam. The mind controls through visualization, the focus, target and projection. The emotions control and regulate the intensity or power of the beam itself from the AEM to the target.

Another important aspect of this operation is to consider the effect upon the target that you, as the operator of the AEM want to achieve. With the conscious or unconscious cooperation of the target the effects are achieved.

There are many ways to visualize the changes you want to bring about. For instance, a change of mind in the target from negative to positive or destructive to benevolent can be imagined. For a change in the environment, the breakdown and neutralization of toxic wastes or radioactivity to render them harmless can be imagined. The Earth, the body, and the mind have many ways to heal themselves and visualizing this can be effective.

When the projector is directed at machinery or devices such as nuclear warheads or other weapons of war, the effect of projecting the neutralization of this machinery provides a way to apply a positive action to an otherwise negative situation. Since machinery is harmless in and of itself, a more effective approach would be to visualize key people in the government and operators of the machinery as developing a more positive image of themselves and the world. "If all of us substituted love for fear in our minds, then there would be no need for weapons of destruction."

However, until love becomes our only motivation, critically serious situations may arise in the near future that would necessitate projecting a beam at a warlike person that would speed up a healing balance for that person. One could also project a negative image of shorting-out the person's ability to react, but that kind of projection is less effective and likely to reflect back on the operator. Keep in mind the truism that, "What goes around, comes around." It's better not to create that kind of negativity for ourselves than to have to deal with what we have created. The golden rule, "Do unto others as you would have done unto you" makes sense when we realize that we are all inextricably connected. Another version of that rule might be, "What you do to others, you are really doing to yourself." The results of our negative actions towards others are not always immediately obvious, but they will manifest sooner or later in some fashion. For those of us well along the spiritual path, we have seen that our negative results are astonishingly rapid and obvious. This is a good sign because it provides us feedback that allows us to modify our behavior so that we can expand and grow at a more rapid pace.

SUMMARY OF OPERATING PROCEDURES

First Procedure

1. Aim the AEM projector at a photograph or a television image, focusing your internal vision until it's clear in your mind.

2. Press the momentary contact switch while visualizing the beam of particles shooting out of the projector. The particles can be visualized as white or golden light (or any other color you choose). Imagine the beam going directly to its target, or through the television system, acting as a UHF carrier wave. The alternative visualization is to imagine the particles disappearing near the projector and reappearing near the target, passing into or through it.

3. Strong emotions add power and intensity to the beam. The mind and emotions of the operator work in conjunction with the device. The process is the same as the principles of positive thinking or visualization that many of us are familiar with.

Second Procedure

1. Without using a photograph or television picture, visualize the target in your mind as clearly as possible. This may require practice.

2. Press the momentary contact switch on the AEM while aiming the projector in the direction of the target. Imagine the beam reaching its target by following geomagnetic field lines or disappearing and reappearing, as above.

3. Use strong emotional desire to add power and intensity to the beam while visualizing the healing of the target or situation as clearly as possible.

Autoelectromags can be powerful tools for growth, and change in our world, as well as devices to promote personal growth. Our world is evolving into one of love and harmony that will endure for many centuries. This is an exciting time of change. Those of us who are living now have chosen to evolve, along with our Earth, into something greater than we have ever been. And, while the demands may be greater on us than they were on our forefathers, the rewards more than repay our extra burden. If we are struggling now or do so in the future we need to remind ourselves of our ultimate goal—a new and better world for ourselves and our children.

DESCRIPTION OF PRACTICE

Practice and doing it are one and the same.

In order to heal the world and it's problems, we must first heal ourselves. It is each individual mind that makes up the mass consciousness that determines what our world is like at any given time. If we want a world of peace, our minds must be peaceful. When enough minds are peaceful, the balance of mass consciousness changes to one of peace and our thoughts manifest on the physical level.

There are two ways we can change this mass consciousness. One is to try to convince others to be peaceful through the use of persuasion, guilt, the media, the AEM and other devices. This may be effective, or it may not. We're all given the gift of free will and anything short of the influence of mass consciousness won't change a mind determined not to change. Therefore, we can't really ever be in control of others unless they consciously or unconsciously hand that control over to us.

However, there is one thing that we are always in control of—ourselves. Taking responsibility for our own thoughts is harder and much more threatening than trying to bully others into changing, but it must be done if we are to change the world. Only when enough of us have changed our own thoughts to love and peace, will the balance of mass consciousness become one of peace and harmony. The practice techniques outlined here, to be used after the basic AEM operation has been mastered, are designed to help us get in tune with ourselves and our bodies in a spirit of love and acceptance for all creation.

Natural Movement

Combining martial arts techniques with the use of an AEM projector requires natural breathing and relaxed ease of movement that comes with practice. The forms and techniques can be improvised from the life experiences of the practitioner. The important part is the feeling of spirit underlying and motivating the action. There's no time to stop and think during the moves. Instinct and inner spirit guide the smoothly liquid flowing of the *ki/chi* energy, which flows through and connects us to all of creation. A humble prayerful attitude with a reverence for all life and creation sets the scenario beforehand. The right actions at the right time follow from this attitude, combined with the inner god spirit that guides us all. Practice of this nature leads to learning and understanding more about ourselves and this guiding spirit.

Shocking thoughts and feelings sometimes surface during early practice sessions with this tool that resembles something that has traditionally been a symbol of violence. But one learns not to hold on to or become attached to any disturbing thoughts. Just observe the thoughts and feelings as they flow through your mind and let them go without being judgmental.

Slow Motion Mirror

One of the most useful devices to use with AEM practice is a full length mirror in which slow motion moves with the projector can be seen. This can be disconcerting at first, but it allows us to see the fluid moving action of the body. We can also see when it's not flowing smoothly. Both are learning experiences. A crystal projector with a lighted crystal can also be used with a mirror in semi-darkness.

The slow motion moves used are often those that are similar to tai chi. If the slowed moves are smooth and flowing, fast action moves will also be liquid gracefulness, expressed with the beauty of a dance. A dance is an excellent way to describe this type of practice. You are the choreographer and whatever movements seem appropriate may be used if you're not familiar with the martial arts. This dance can be practiced anywhere, without a mirror when one is not available. The important ingredient is letting a sense of spiritual energy and love guide the movements while using any of the AEM projectors.

The Grip

Movements with the AEMs can use right or left-hand grips with a two-handed grip in some moves. If you're right-handed, try using your left, or vice versa. This is good practice for developing dexterity and balance. Smooth, balanced motion is the key to practice with any style of crystal projector.

AEM Projector Thoughts

What we really think about guns and hostility is going to come to the surface of our minds during practice with crystal projectors. Anything can happen at this point. A pacifist may be surprised to find hostile thoughts and feelings that were affecting the world around him or her surfacing. It's possible to heal these thoughts by acknowledging them without judgment and then letting them go. On the other hand, a hostile lonely person, who has relied on having projectile guns around for false security, may find a sense of peace and balance that provides a strong inner security, along with a sense of oneness with the world.

Practice with crystal projectors allows people to look at their feelings about themselves and the rest of the world. Facing those feelings can allow them the freedom of choice to be at-one, lovingly, with the inner self and the world.

Most people really want peace, harmony and happiness when

they look deeply into their inner beings. The AEM projectors are a tool for finding personal balance that then begins radiating outward, providing good energy to the universe.

The AEM is a tool, a symbol for achieving our highest ideals. The goal is for our projectors to reflect the new higher spirituality that we are growing into. As we know, everything around us reflects what we are. When our guns have developed into spiritual tools, as the AEMs have done, we will know that we have grown.

Combining martial arts techniques with the use of the AEM involves using slow motion moves while focusing energy through the projector and concentrating on inner spiritual development. Below are descriptions of two typical practice sessions with AEMs to give you a frame of reference for developing your own techniques.

The first scenario demonstrates how you might use martial arts movements or dance with the AEM in an outdoor rock garden to expand your awareness of the harmony of nature.

The curving flagstone pathway is faintly lighted from the moon above, with pinpricks of starlight visible above the lush foliage of surrounding trees. White circles of quartz rocks glow in the night, while vines form shadows that trail downward from the hedge surrounding the secluded rock garden. Individual plants are silent sentinels in their rock circles.

Two cats move in the serene garden of the night. The faint whisper of their bodies brushing against leaves gently breaks the silence. They freeze their motion, the eyes of each seeking movement in the still darkness.

Fragrances from flowers and growing plants hang in the blackness of the silent air. The cats' seeking eyes see nothing, but they catch the scent of another close by. A human figure appears out of the invisible night on the path in the center of the garden, like one of their own.

While the serenity of the night garden remains undisturbed, the cats stare in fascination as the black-clad figure wearing a shoulder holster turns a clockwise circle in slow motion silence. The human moves like an animal or a bird.

A shadow flows across the mirror of water in the stone birdbath as the form completes the circle. The human's arms are in front during the turn, bent at elbows in blocking positions. One arm and hand are slightly lower than chin height, the other just above the navel. Each forearm is six to eight inches in front of the body. The figure's feet move crab-like in backward, sideways steps during the turn with the left elbow coming back even with the side of the body as the right hand moves from chin level downward to-

wards the left armpit.

The right hand grasps the grip of the AEM, pulling it from the shoulder holster in an upward diagonal half-circle arc. Then the left hand comes forward at heart level to grasp the right hand and projector grip. Knees bend slowly into a crouch at the end of the draw. Moonlight, reflected on the copper barrel, shines through the crystal tip of the AEM as the form straightens up to full height.

The figure turns the projector upside-down, with a hand on each end of the barrel, then holds it up to the sky. The outline of the AEM, with the handgrip pointed up, looks like a pipe being offered to the Great Spirit in prayer. That's exactly what it is.

Laying the AEM in the center of a stone circle as an offering to the Mother Earth, the dark form kneels at the circle of rocks, breathing slowly and deeply with four exhalations and inhalations that reach out through the stars to the depths of the universe and return the same way from the far reaches of space.

The figure then sits in the still silence while the cats move forward to examine this being more closely. One cat crawls into the human's lap while the other rubs against the human's side. All three are joined in a balanced harmony of spirit.

The second scenario of a practice session demonstrates how an AEM can be used for a healing of the Earth.

The view over the barrel of the AEM shows a heavy drift of wet snow with green stalks futilely striving to reach the sun. A clump of irises, crushed by the snow, is the target to be healed by the AEM. The human feels unconditional love for the Earth while visualizing a beam of blue-white light shooting outward from the crystal in the copper barrel of the projector. The life energy of the Earth flowing up from the ground infuses the operator's body while the energy of the universe courses down through his head. A visualization of the beam of energy reaches the roots at the base of the flower clump. The flow of healing energy spins downward through the plant's roots seeking the life force of the Earth, then spirals upwards seeking the sun. When the vision of healthy blooming flowers completely forms in the operator's mind, the healing of the plant is accomplished.

The healing technique outlined above can be expanded to include a large area or even the entire Earth. The principles used know no limit of size or distance. The only limit is the scope of our minds.

Chapter 6

AUTOELECTROMAG (AEM) I

The heart of the Earth, the place where souls meet.

THE EARTH IS A REFLECTION OF OURSELVES

If we only had access to the secret sciences of ancient Earth civilizations or communication with advanced extraterrestrial civilizations, we could learn to solve so many of our earthly problems. This statement has been repeated often during the last thirty years. Now we do have some knowledge of both through new inventions, science, channeling and regressions. We've finally found what we've been seeking and learned that what we sought resided in ourselves all along. Over and over again we've been told to look within ourselves for the answers. That knowledge may not be as romantically dramatic as our dreams, but it's proving to be real and usable. When we take the trouble to look within, all the answers are there because of our connection to the Source.

It's hard to believe that such simple, yet sophisticated devices as psionic generators and the autoelectromags can be as effective as they are. The only requirement is that we put forth the effort to spiritually develop ourselves. Is it worth the effort? Yes, it is. It offers us hope for a future that doesn't include repeating our past in endless cycles. Instead, we can go on to the next step in our evolution. Overnight success in changing ourselves and our world for the better is rare, but at least we can be confident of ultimate success instead of the doomsday scenarios sometimes predicted. The autoelectromag has proven to be an effective tool in bringing about the changes we desire by amplifying the energy of our thoughts to enhance evolution on an individual and global scale.

Why?—Why Not?

Why should we work so hard on ourselves? The main goal is to provide balance and raise the vibrational level of the Earth by changing ourselves and our perceptions. Influences we see as being outside ourselves are the key to our personal spiritual development. These forces are not outside ourselves at all, because we are only able to perceive that which we are. Therefore, the only way to balance what we see as negative forces is to expand our consciousness to a higher vibrational level that will enable us to visualize a greater good materializing (i.e., thought creates form). We can do this by using the inherent power of our human consciousness. This balancing force can be applied on a local level, a national level, an international level and even an extraterrestrial level.

There are some ethical issues we may need to resolve before we can release ourselves from the paralyzing inaction that causes so much of our frustration. It's time that we take responsibility for ourselves, our government and our world. To do that we need to take an honest look at what kind of world we're creating with our thoughts and then change our thoughts to create the kind of world we really want. In this light, adaptations of traditional weapons into crystal tools of light and learning are offered to inspire a higher consciousness for us all.

This chapter includes the early autoelectromag projectors and the directions for building them. The projectors are a combination of a psionic black box and a crystal rod, as explained in the previous chapter.

PREPARING FOR AEM USE

Before using your AEM, you may wish to step up your own energy by forming and shaping a ball of energy between the hands. To do this, both hands are used in movements similar to making a snowball. The ball is visualized as a miniature sun formed from the healing energy flowing between the palms.

This energy flow, sometimes called *ki* or *chi*, is the overall energy field or unifying force of the universe. Peace and healing can be expressed by creating projectors that use this energy, which comes directly from the Source.

The flow of energy is then channeled through the AEM projector to radiate outward. A natural balanced circuit exists when a crystal tool is energized this way. The universal connection that's already operating begins to radiate more energy when a human operator channels it in an energy sphere that can be expanded to encompass the Earth or the whole universe.

Energizing the AEM operator can also be done another way. The sphere of energy can be formed and shaped with the hands, as above, with the energy visualized in the shape of the human aura. An AEM can then be used to project a beam of energy out of the intensified aura. This beam can be imagined as traveling to any area, at any distance, instantly. The effects of the beam as it reaches its target are determined by the purpose of the individual operator. If the target is an Earth healing spot, the effects and dispersion of energy can be left up to the Earth itself.

PSI-SUB AEM

The psi-sub (psionic-subatomic) AEM is built using the casing from an electric drill. These are fairly easy to acquire at garage sales, or perhaps you have a burnt-out drill that can be used. This model was the first primitive prototype of the AEM built in 1980.

Materials:

A. Copper coupler, 3/4"

B. Quartz crystal, about 2" long, at least 1/2" in diameter

C. Leather strip, enough to wrap around exposed copper pipe for insulation

D. Putty or plastic caulking compound

E. Copper tube, 3/4" diameter, approximately 10" long

F. Plastic housing from an electric drill gun (with trigger switch, if possible)

G. Solid heavy gauge copper wire, 12" long

H. Spring loaded electrical switch or trigger from the drill

I. Copper end cap, 3/4"

J. Two capacitors, any size

K. One on/off volume switch (rheostat)

L. Insulated copper wire, several short lengths (4" to 5")

M. Assortment of copper or brass screws for both wood and metal

N. Flat spray paint, any color

O. Strips of copper mesh or leather (shim for crystal)

P. Plastic electrical tape

Q. Aluminum foil or duct tape to cover caulked areas

R. Instant bonding glue to mount A and I

Construction:

The Barrel Assembly

1. Cut a 10" length of 3/4" copper tubing (E).

2. Wrap approximately two feet of heavy solid copper wire around the outside of the pipe to form a spiral (G). Bend the spiral to a smaller diameter so it will fit inside the copper tube.

3. Attach an 8" length of insulated copper wire (L) to each end of the spiral.

4. Place the copper cap (I) on the tube (E) and drill a small hole

in the tube just in front of the cap on top of the pipe for one lead from the coil to slide through. Drill another hole as per diagram for the other lead about 2-1/2" from end cap.

5. Insert the coil and leads into the tube for a tight fit and pull one lead through each hole.
6. Glue the end cap (I) in place at the coil end of the tube.
7. Mount the crystal (B) in copper coupler (A) using instant bonding glue and copper mesh or leather shims (O), if necessary.
8. Glue coupler (A) with mounted crystal to copper tube (E).

NOTE: The barrel assembly is complete, except for mounting and insulating with leather on the exposed section, and electrical tape on the inside covered part (inside the drill housing).

The Drill Housing and Electrical Wiring

1. Take out the screws and disassemble the drill, saving the trigger switch (H), the plastic housing (F), and the screws to reassemble after adaptation.
2. Place the copper barrel assembly against the inside of half of the drill housing.
3. Since the round plastic braces (for the motor) are not quite the right shape for the copper barrel to point straight out at the right angle, cut the braces to fit the barrel. This can be done with a saw, tin snips, soldering iron, or other available implements, so that the barrel will fit tight and straight.
4. Wrap the inside area of the barrel with electrical tape (P) so that it fits tightly. It can also be attached in any other way you think is suitable.
5. Test it in place by putting both halves of the housing back together for a good fit. If it fits, go on to the next step.
6. Tie the two leads (L) to small capacitors (J), one on each end of each lead.
7. Drill out a hole in the butt of the housing.

8. Insert the on/off dial (K). If the dial fits properly, attach a wire from the capacitor of one lead to one connection on the dial and wrap the connection with electrical tape (P).

9. Run a wire from the other connection on the dial to one connection on the trigger switch (H) and attach firmly.

10. The other lead wire from the trigger switch should then be attached to the extra capacitor and lead wire of the barrel housing.

NOTE: At this point, the wiring is complete. Make sure the connections are stable and cover them with electrical tape or solder. Ascertain that there are no crossed wires in the circuit before installing permanently into the housing.

Final Assembly

1. Double check everything that has been done so far.

2. Reassemble the drill housing with the barrel and wiring inside and trigger switch in its place.

3. Tighten all the screws attaching the two halves of the housing.

4. Putty or plastic caulking compound (D) can be used to cover the screw holes and make a tight seal where the barrel protrudes from the front of the housing. Then cover the caulking with aluminum foil tape or duct tape (Q).

5. A strip of leather, spiral-wrapped, or a single piece of leather can be glued to cover the exposed barrel (C).

6. Any other indentations can be filled with caulking compound and/or taped with duct tape.

7. Cover the leather on the barrel with masking tape before painting to protect the leather.

8. Spray paint the gun exterior (N). Black or silver is nice, but any color can be used.

NOTE: Make sure the paint is dry before proceeding to the next step.

9. Be sure the dial (K) and trigger switch (H) still operate freely.

Comments:

The psi-sub (psionic-subatomic) projector was built almost entirely from salvaged scrap except for the copper fittings and quartz crystal. This model is economical to build and can provide as powerful a learning experience as the later, more sophisticated models.

PSI- SUB AEM INTERIOR

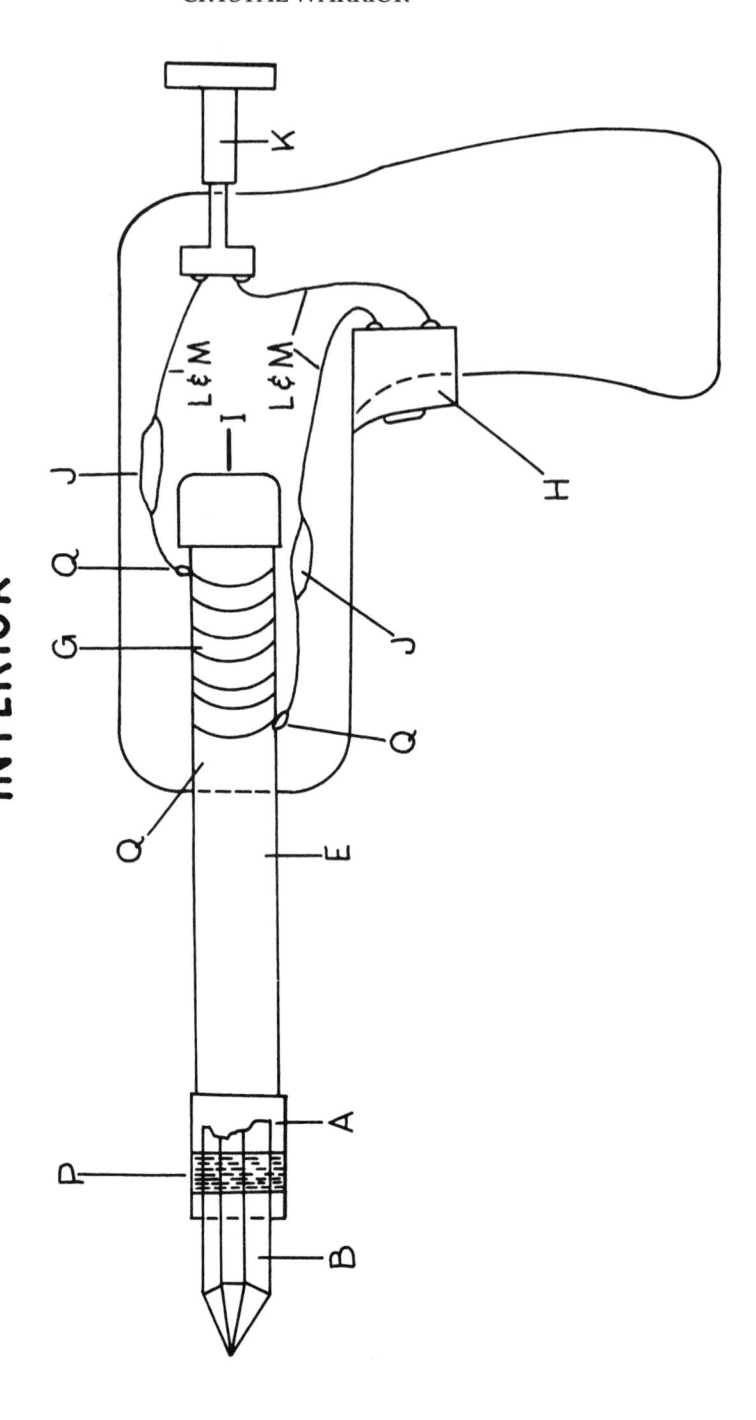

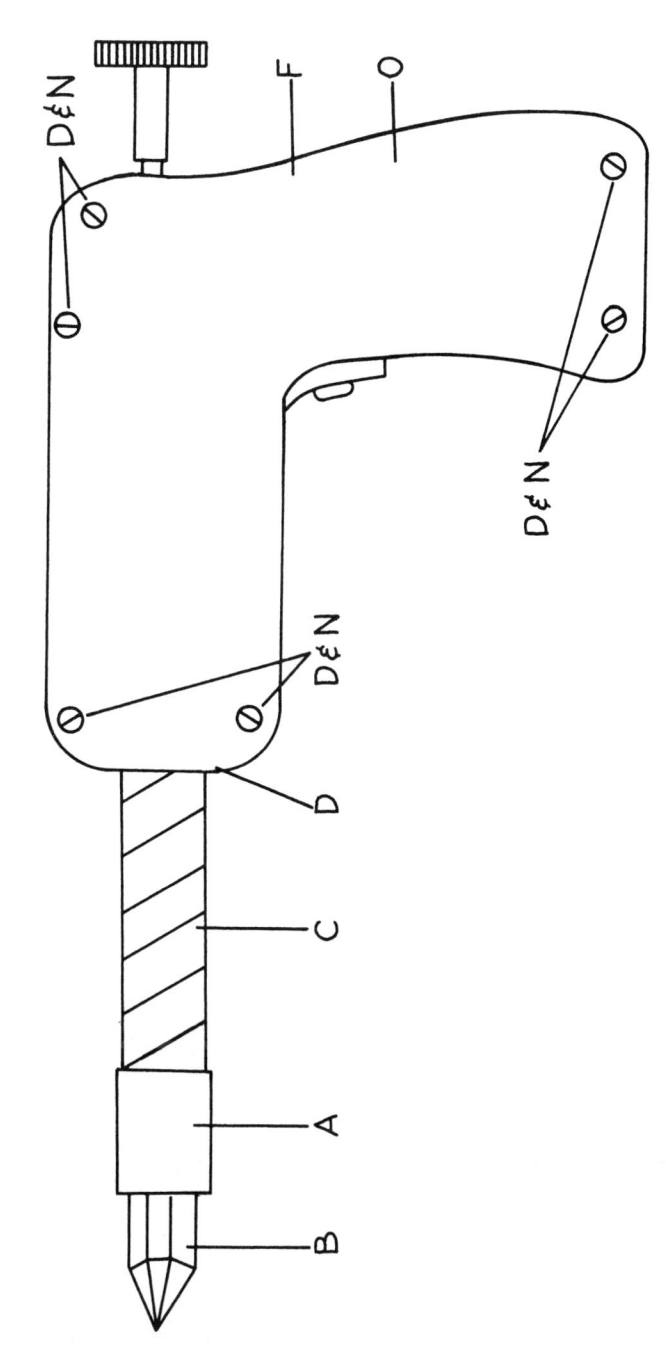

PSI- SUB AEM
EXTERIOR

AEM BEAMER

The AEM beamer model resulted from the need to reduce the early models of the AEMs to a smaller, more manageable, size and streamline them for easier usage. The beamer is easy to carry in a pocket or a purse. Like the reduced-size crystal rods in the books *Crystal Power and Crystal Spirit*, this smaller version of the AEM can be carried and used at all times.

Materials:

A. Copper reducer, 3/4" to 1/2"

B. Copper coupler, 3/4"

C. Quartz crystal, about 2" long by 1/2" diameter and enough leather or copper mesh strips to shim it tightly into the coupler

D. Copper tube, 3/4" by 5" long

E. Solid heavy gauge copper wire, 24"

F. Copper end cap, 3/4"

G. Assorted brass or copper screws

H. Hardwood or pine block, 1" thick, 4" x 5" to cut for projector grip

I. Switch, spring loaded push-button type

J. Two capacitors, can be from an old radio

K. Two insulated copper wires, 8" long

L. Leather strip wide enough to cover barrel in one piece with seam at bottom

M. Instant bonding glue

Construction:

The Barrel Unit

1. Insert the crystal (C) into copper reducer (A), using thin strips of copper mesh or leather wrapped around the crys-

tal as shims. Glue the crystal in place.

2. Glue the 3/4" end of the reducer (A) into the 3/4" coupler (B).
3. Glue the coupler (B) to the end of the 5" long 3/4" diameter tube (D).
4. Bend about 2' of heavy solid copper wire into a spiral (E) and attach an 8" length of insulated copper wire (K) to each end.
5. Insert the spiral (E), curving to the right, into the tube. It should fit tightly.
6. Drill a hole just in front of the end cap (F) in the copper tube (D).
7. Pull the two insulated wires (K) through the hole.
8. Glue the copper end cap (F) in place.

NOTE: Now we have completed the barrel unit and should be ready to begin on the wooden grip. The copper barrel unit will be ready to mount after a flat leather piece (L) is wrapped around the copper tube (D) and glued with the seam at the bottom.

The Wooden Projector Grip

1. Draw a rough outline of the grip you want on a 4" by 5" by 1" thick board (H).
2. Cut out a rough grip with a jigsaw.
3. Cut a v-shaped notch in the top of the grip for the barrel to rest on.
4. Sand thoroughly with a sander, rounding all edges.

Final Assembly

1. Draw an outline of the push-button switch (I) on the wooden pistol grip (H) at the trigger position.
2. Use an electric drill to drill out an area large enough for the switch to be inserted in a suitable position.

3. Mount the switch (I). Switch must be stable and spring action should work freely. This may require some careful remounting in order to secure it properly. When drilling out for the trigger, make sure a hole goes all the way through to the top of the grip for wires to pass through later on.

4. Drill out at least a 1" by 1/4" slot in the top of the grip for the capacitors and wiring running from the barrel to the grip.

NOTE: During the final stage, you should have a completed barrel assembly. Attach the two lead wires (K) to each end of the copper spiral (E).

5. Attach a small capacitor from an old radio (J) to each lead wire (K).

6. Attach the lead wires (K) to the push-button switch (I).

7. Tape wire connections with electrical tape.

8. Drill two holes in the bottom ends of the grip and drill mounting holes to match in the barrel assembly.

9. Mount barrel on wooden grip (H) with copper or brass screws (G).

10. Tighten barrel assembly to wooden grip.

11. If the barrel doesn't fit the notch in the projector grip exactly, use leather strips to fill in the spaces. Push them in with a knife or screwdriver.

12. To finish the beamer off, use a coat of lemon oil or furniture polish.

Autoelectromag (AEM) I 45

AEM BEAMER INTERIOR

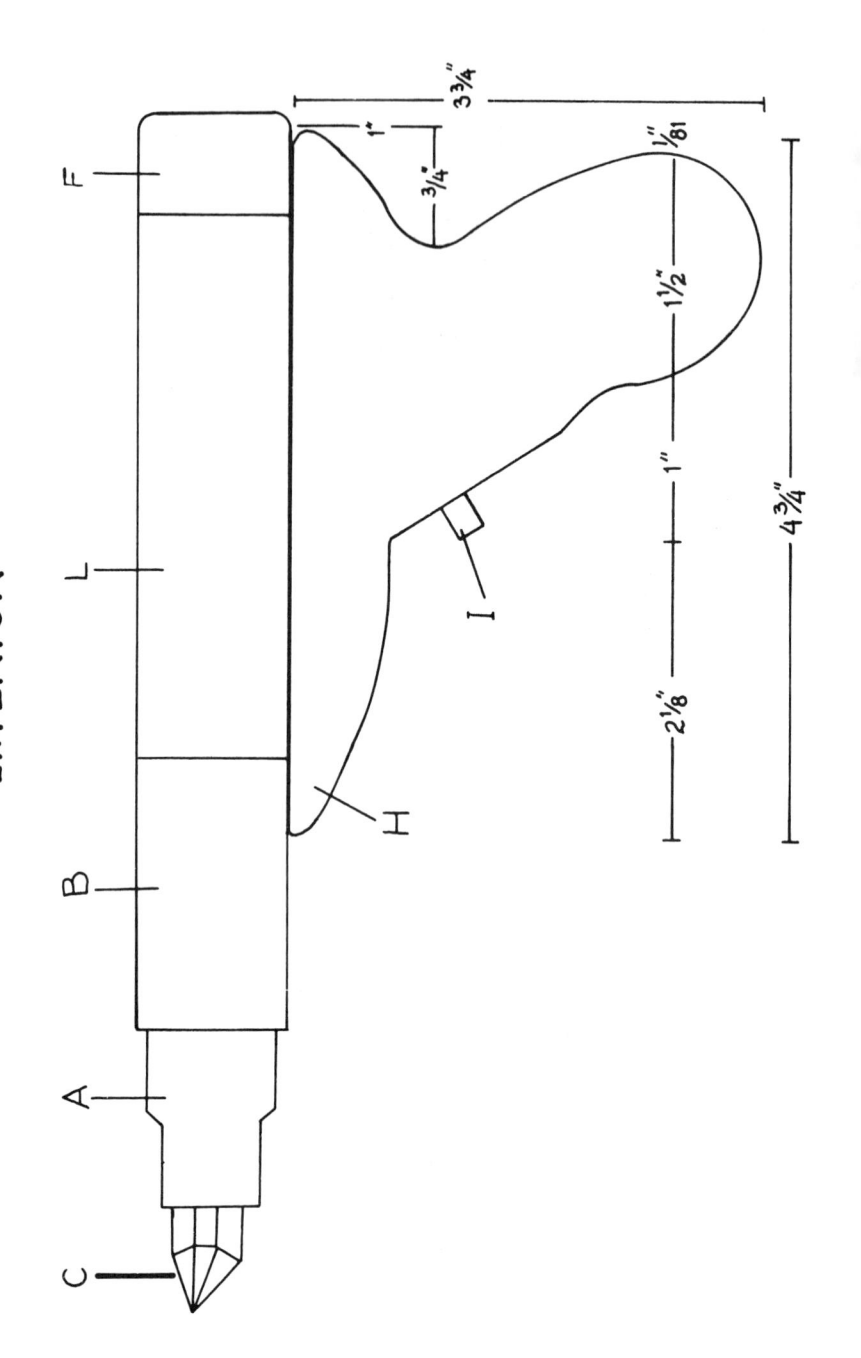

AEM BEAMER EXTERIOR

Chapter 7

AUTOELECTROMAG (AEM) II

And ye shall know the truth, and the truth shall make you free.

John, VIII: 32

The newest autoelectromags are refined versions of the earlier models that operate in the same manner. Included in this chapter are directions for building the space age AEM, the x-tal AEM, and the mini AEM.

These models were all developed to expand the scope of the knowledge that we and others gained by building and using the original autoelectromags. In building any of these projectors, we think you'll find that the process of working with crystals in this manner will change and expand your view of the universe and your part in it.

SPACE AGE AUTOELECTROMAG

Autoelectromags came into being between 1980 and 1986. The space age autoelectromag is one of the latest models. It's also one of the most difficult to build, but well worth the effort.

Building any of the AEMs is a learning experience. The space age AEM is another tool for learning where we are, what we are and what we are developing into—in short, learning about ourselves. A regular gun doesn't teach a person much. A crystal energy projector can show us our thoughts, emotions, spirit and act as a gauge of our awareness that we are one and interconnected with all creation. There have been stories of magical rods, knives and swords. Maybe what we need for our present society are magical guns.

Materials:

A. Copper ring shim, 3/4" diameter

B. 3/4" copper coupling

C. 3/4" copper tubing, 1" length

D. 3/4" to 1/2" copper reducer

E. 1/2" copper tubing, 1" length

F. 3/4" to 1/2" copper reducer

G. 3/4" copper coupling

H. 3/4" copper tubing, 7-1/2" length

I. 3/4" copper cap

J. 7-1/2" piece of leather approximately 3" wide

K. Quartz crystal, slightly less than 3/4" x 1-1/2" length—double termination

L. Quartz crystal, slightly less than 3/4" x 1-1/2" length—single termination

M. 12 round ceramic magnets, 1/2" diameter wrapped in copper mesh

N. Momentary contact push-button switch

O. 8–10 gauge solid copper wire, 24" wound into a coil

P. 1/2" wide strip of electrical tape

Q. 1/2" wide strip of copper mesh or copper foil tape

R. 1-1/2" brass screw

S. Wooden pistol handgrip with 1/2" slot (we used a Thompson submachine gun handgrip from Auto Ordnance Corporation)

T. 1-1/2" brass screw

U. Small gauge insulated copper wire (connects switch to coil)

V. 1" length of 3/4" diameter copper tubing

W. Holes drilled for switch and wires

X. Holes for barrel mounting screw

Y. Single termination crystal slightly less than 1/2" diameter (optional)

Z. Holes at each end of (H) for mounting screws and hole for wires from coil to switch

Construction:

All parts of the barrel assembly should be cut and fitted together first without glue or the interior parts. This will ensure they fit properly and allow for adjustments before final assembly. (See diagram—parts A through I.)

Three holes (Z) need to be drilled in the copper tube (H). The two for the mounting screws should be slightly smaller in diameter than the screws are. The third hole for the wires needs to be large enough for the wires to go through. These holes are easier to deal with if the projector grip hole (W) is drilled first.

The Projector Grip

The holes for the barrel mounting (X) need to be drilled slightly larger than the diameter of the mounting screws. The hole for the momentary contact switch (W) needs to be large enough for the switch to be pushed into, leaving only the push-button exposed. The longer part of hole (W) needs to be drilled downward to meet the other part of the hole drilled in for the switch. This hole only needs to be large enough for the two wires from the switch to the copper coil. Now that the pistol grip is drilled, we have a guide or template for drilling the barrel assembly.

The Barrel Assembly

Slide the end cap (I) onto the longer tubing (H) and slide the first copper coupling (G) onto the other end on this tube. Do not glue any of these together yet.

The barrel assembly can now be set in the slot on top of the pistol grip. A nail or thin punch can be used to reach through the screw holes (X) to mark the two spots to drill on the barrel assembly. Remember to drill these two holes smaller than the diameter of the screws so they will fit tightly to hold the barrel on the pistol grip when it's mounted later on. You can now see where to drill the hole in the barrel for the two insulated wires (U) that run from the copper coil (O) to the push button trigger switch (N).

Now that the holes (Z) are drilled, take the coupling and cap back off and prepare to put together the complete barrel assembly. The coil, which is made from the 24" length of 8 or 10 gauge solid copper wire, can be formed by wrapping the wire around a 6" length of 1/2" diameter copper tubing, then pulling the copper tube out of the coil. The small gauge insulated copper wires should be cut over 12" long, so they'll be easier to work with. During the process they have to be fed through the hole in the barrel as the coil is pushed into the back of the barrel. Later on, they'll have to fed through the hole in the pistol grip as well. Each wire should be attached to each end of the copper coil, either by soldering or being twisted together and secured with electrical tape.

The coil is then wrapped with electrical tape, enough so it will fit snugly inside the back of the barrel. The insulated wires are fed into the barrel and through the wire hole that was previously drilled. The coil is pushed in as the wires are pulled through the hole. The end of the coil should be even with the back end of the tube. The end cap (I) can now be glued in place with instant bonding glue. Wrap the magnets (M) with copper mesh, copper foil tape or electrical tape so they will slide into the front end of the tube (H) and fit snugly in front of the coil. The first coupling (G) can now be glued on the front end of the tube. Wrap the single termination quartz crystal (L) with copper mesh or copper tape at the base for a shim to make it fit tightly inside the copper coupling (G). The short piece of copper tubing (V) must also be able to slide into the copper coupling (G). Quite often, the pressure from this piece of tubing will hold the crystal securely in place without glue. If not, the crystal and mesh or tape shim can still be glued in. The piece of tubing (V) can then be glued into the coupling.

The first reducer (F) is now glued onto the end of the copper tubing (V) sticking out of the coupling, the large end of the reducer should fit tightly against the coupling with no large crack or the tubing inside showing.

The 1/2" piece of tubing (E) is glued into the 1/2" end of the reducer (F). The other reducer (D) is glued to the tubing (E) as well. It should fit snugly so the inside piece of tubing (E) doesn't show. The next piece of copper tubing (C) is then glued into the reducer (D). Now, the last coupling (B) can be glued on the other end of the copper tubing (C). It, also, should fit snugly against the reducer so that there is no wide gap showing any of the copper tubing.

Mounting the Double Termination Crystal

Wrap the double termination quartz crystal (K) with copper mesh or copper foil tape (Q) so it fits securely into the coupling (B) with part of the crystal inside the tubing (C). This will leave room for the copper ring shim (A) to be glued inside the coupling (B) so it's flush with the end. One tip of the crystal will just barely be sticking through the back of the copper ring shim.

NOTE: For a spacier look, a third, single termination crystal (Y) slightly less than 1/2" in diameter can be mounted inside the copper ring shim (A) with copper tape and glue.

The Leather Wrap

The leather piece (J) should be wrapped and glued around the long length of the tubing so the seam is at the bottom. It should cover only the tubing between the copper cap (I) and the first coupling (G). Some small areas of leather may need to be cut away from the holes on the bottom of the tubing (Z). This may not be necessary if the seam is centered over the holes.

The Pistol Grip

Now that the barrel assembly is together in one piece, we can go back to the pistol grip which we drilled holes in earlier.

Push the two insulated wires hanging from the barrel assembly down through the hole (W) so they come out the front where the switch will be installed. Line up the mounting holes in the barrel with the pistol grip holes (X). Attach the barrel assembly with the brass screws (R and T).

We have an almost complete assembly. The insulated wires (U) are sticking down through the hole (W) and out the front of the projector grip. These can be attached to the push button switch, one to each contact. They can be soldered on or the wires twisted together and wrapped with small pieces of electrical tape. (The wires may need to be cut shorter at this point.)

Insert the switch into the hole (W). This can be a pressure fit even if the base of the switch needs to be wrapped with electrical tape as a shim or spacer. If more space is needed, the hole can be drilled larger.

NOTE: Optional in-line capacitors can be attached to the switch wires if desired. Early AEMs used these, but later ones did not.

Comments:

More than a crystal tool for self-development, this AEM is a real work of art. The design and the parts used reflect this. A display stand or wall rack could be built for it. Other finishing touches can also be added. Ours has a solid silver lightning bolt inset in the back of the pistol grip, below the copper end cap. It also has a turquoise stone in a silver cap inset at the very bottom of the handgrip. There are other personal touches you might think of to add to yours. The wooden handgrip can be rubbed with an oil-type wood treatment to bring out the beauty of the natural wood grain and preserve the wood. This AEM is a common size that will fit many of the standard holsters made by manufacturers as well.

SPACE AGE AUTOELECTROMAG

INTERIOR VIEW

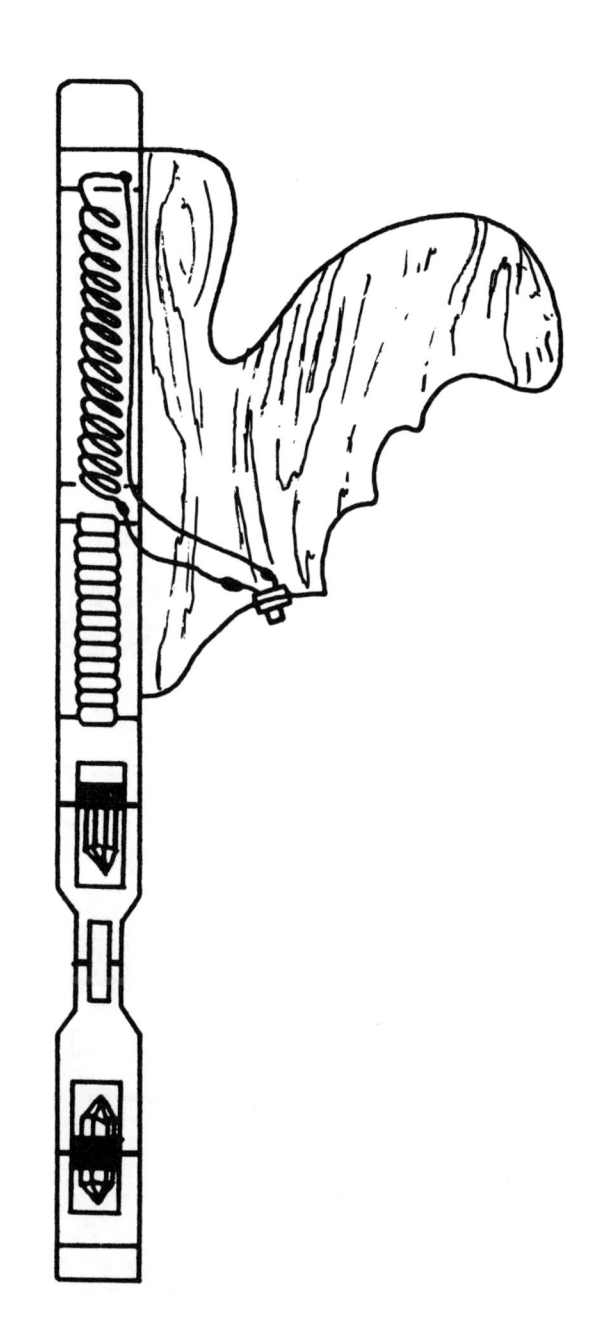

SPACE AGE AUTOELECTROMAG

EXTERIOR VIEW

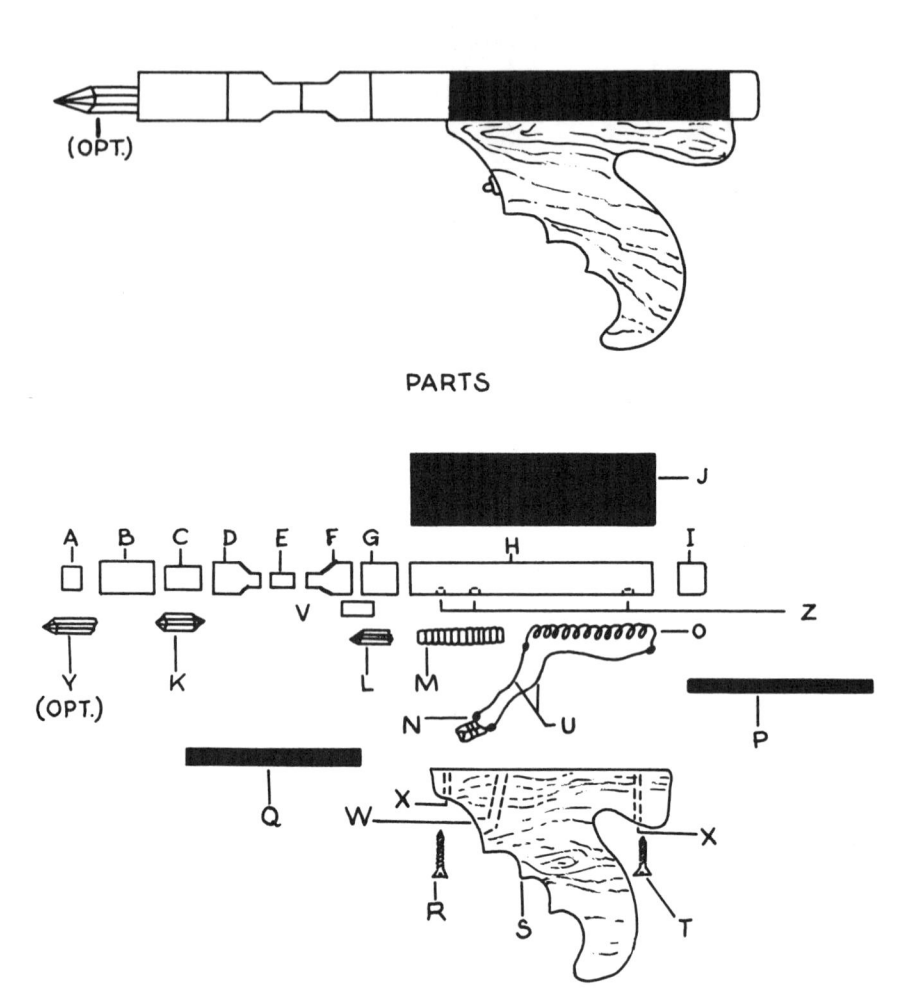

PARTS

X-TAL AUTOELECTROMAG

The x-tal autoelectromag's stock is one that you construct yourself out of a block of wood. It's somewhat less complicated than the space age AEM to build, but is just as effective for self-development.

Materials:

A. Copper reducer, 3/4" to 1/2" diameter (3/4" end should fit inside 3/4" copper coupler)

B. Quartz crystal, 3/4" diameter by 2" length

C. Copper foil tape or leather as shim for crystal and switch

D. Instant bonding glue

E. Copper coupler, 3/4" diameter

F. 3/4" copper pipe, 12" length

G. Leather—12" length by 3" wide, wrapped and glued with the seam at the bottom of the barrel

H. Copper wire spiral coil, 8 to 12 gauge—24" length

I. 3/4" copper end cap

J. Mounting screws, 2-1/4" long

K. Stock—cut from a 2" x 11" x 6" piece of wood to fit barrel and operator's hand

L. Trigger guard—brass or copper strap held on with screws, 1/2" wide, 6" long

M. Momentary contact switch for trigger

N. Lead wires connecting switch and ends of coil—copper, insulated

O. 2 capacitors

Construction:

The materials used in the construction of the autoelectromags, like the early psionic-radionic machines, seem to take second place to the pattern and connections. Some of the early machines were actually built out of cardboard instead of the electronic parts. Surprisingly, they functioned as well as the actual machines. This explains why there can be so much improvisation on construction and materials to suit individual builders and operators.

The Barrel Assembly

The main section of the barrel assembly is built with a 12" length of copper pipe with a 3/4" diameter (F). The copper coil (H) can be formed around a piece of 1/2" diameter copper pipe. This is then taken off and enlarged to fit snugly inside the barrel assembly. A small hole for the lead wires is drilled several inches in front of the end that the copper cap (I) will be mounted on. The lead wires are attached to the ends of the coil and the connections can be wrapped with one layer of electrical tape. The coil is then inserted into the barrel with the lead wires running out through the small hole in the bottom. The end cap can be glued on with instant bonding glue after the coil is in place.

Mounting the Crystal

The quartz crystal (B) is inserted into the copper reducer (A). You may need to use leather or copper foil tape (C) as a shim around it to make it fit securely before gluing it in. The copper coupler (E) is glued to the end of the copper pipe. Next, the copper reducer (A) with the mounted crystal is glued inside the copper coupler. There are two kinds of copper reducers (3/4" to 1/2"). Make sure you buy the one that has the 3/4" end small enough to fit inside the copper coupler. You are now ready to apply a leather or shrink tube covering (G) to the copper pipe (F) between the end cap and the copper coupler. If leather is used, it should be cut in one piece and glued at the bottom where the hole for the lead wires is. When you have done this, the barrel assembly is complete.

The Stock

The stock (K) is cut from a pine 2" x 6" using a jigsaw to cut the outline penciled in on the board. The length of the piece is 11" and the height is 5-1/4" (see diagram for individual measurements). The corners of the handgrip, as well as the rest of the stock, are rounded and sanded. A hole slightly larger than the trigger switch is drilled in the handgrip (see diagram). Another hole is drilled down to meet it from the top of the stock to accommodate the lead wires and capacitors. It can be drilled at either a 90 degree or 45 degree angle. A v-shaped groove is cut in the top of the stock for the barrel assembly to rest on. This groove is 5/8" wide by 1/4" deep. The barrel is then set in the stock with the lead wires running through the hole to where the trigger switch (M) will be. The two holes for the mounting screws (J) are drilled. The holes in the stock are slightly larger than the diameter of the screws. The holes in the stock can be used as a guide to mark the barrel and then two holes drilled in the barrel that are slightly smaller than the diameter of the 2-1/4" long screws.

Final Assembly

The screws are inserted to attach the barrel to the stock. The capacitors and switch are attached to the lead wires and the trigger switch can be pressure fitted into the hole in the handgrip. A shim can be made by wrapping electrical tape around the base of the switch to make it fit snugly.

The trigger guard is made of a 1/2" wide piece of brass or copper, 6" long (L). It is bent to fit on the stock as shown. A small hole in each end is drilled for the mounting screws.

The unit can be disassembled and the stock stained and varnished before final assembly. This device can be a work of art, as well as a crystal tool, if care is used in its construction. While the device is primarily an energy, thought and emotion projector, it can also make a nice display when not being used, if it's mounted on a finished wooden wall plaque.

X-TAL AEM

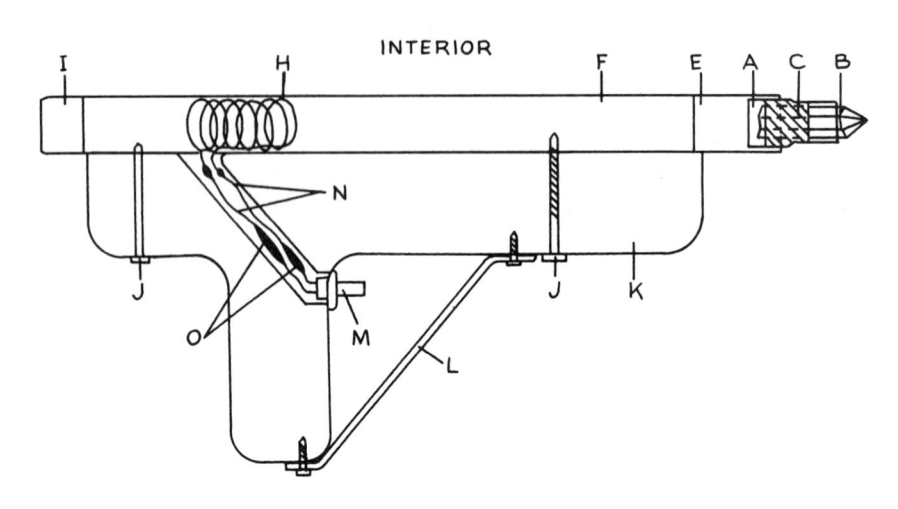

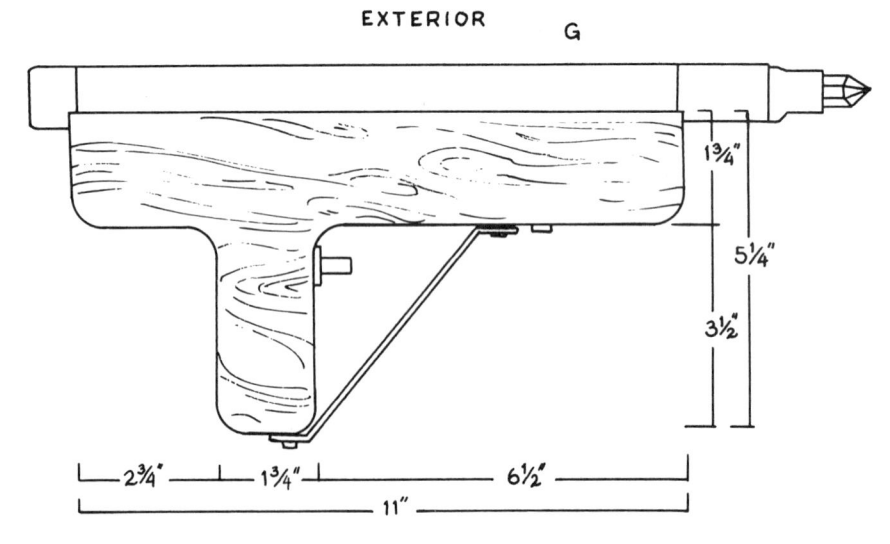

INTERIOR

EXTERIOR

1¾"
5¼"
3½"
2¾"
1¾"
6½"
11"

MINI AUTOELECTROMAG

The mini autoelectromag is the smallest version of the AEMs and can be carried even more conveniently than the AEM beamer in a purse or pocket. Despite its small size the mini produces a projection of energy every bit as powerful as the larger versions.

Materials:

A. Copper coupler, 1/2"

B. Quartz crystal, less than 1/2" diameter x 1" to 1-1/2" length

C. 1/2" copper pipe, 3-1/2" length

D. Shrink tube covering (or leather)

E. Copper wire for spiral coil, medium gauge, 8" to 12"

F. Copper end cap, 1/2"

G. Projector grip stock, 3" length by 2-1/2" height, hard or soft wood

H. Momentary contact switch for trigger

I. Insulated copper wire leads from switch to coil

J. 2 capacitors

K. Two 1/2" copper tubing clamps

L. 4 small screws

M. Leather or copper foil tape shim for crystal

N. Instant bonding glue

O. Oil or stain and varnish finish for stock

Construction:

The Barrel Assembly

The copper coupling (A) is glued to the copper pipe (C) first. The quartz crystal (B) is then glued with instant bonding glue inside the coupling after being wrapped with leather or copper tape (M) to make it fit snugly. A small hole is drilled in the bottom of the barrel

(C) for the insulated wire leads from coil to switch. The coil (E) with insulated leads (I) attached is inserted into the back of the barrel with the leads running out through the hole in the bottom of the barrel. The copper end cap (F) can now be glued on. Two in-line capacitors can be attached to the insulated wire leads. The barrel assembly is now complete.

The Projector Grip Stock

The projector grip can be made of hard or soft wood, but soft wood is easier to work with. It is cut from a 1" thick piece of wood, 3" long by 2-1/2" high (G). The bottom piece of the handgrip is 1-1/2" by 1" (see diagram). The area for the trigger switch (H) is drilled out for the switch to fit into and a smaller hole is drilled upward for the leads to run through to the coil in the barrel. The wooden grip can be finished with oil or, for a more polished look, with wood stain and varnish (O).

The barrel assembly is held on with two 1/2" copper tubing clamps using a total of four screws, two on each side (L). The 3" top of the projector grip stock may need a v-notch or rounding out for the barrel assembly to fit more neatly.

The momentary contact switch trigger can be the kind that is attached with screws or the type that may be wrapped with copper tape as a shim and glued or pressure fitted in the hole drilled in the pistol grip earlier. All wiring should be soldered or twisted together securely and wrapped with electrical tape. This project is complete when the wires have been connected and the trigger switch mounted.

Autoelectromag (AEM) II 61

MINI AEM

EXTERIOR VIEW

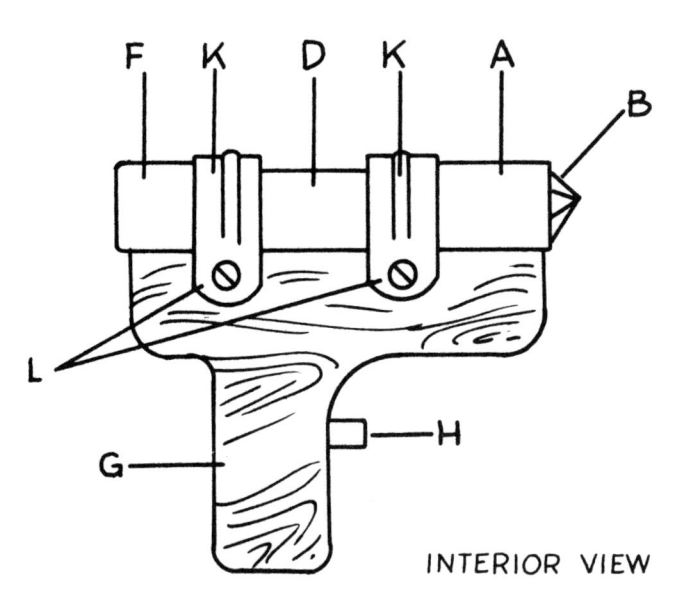

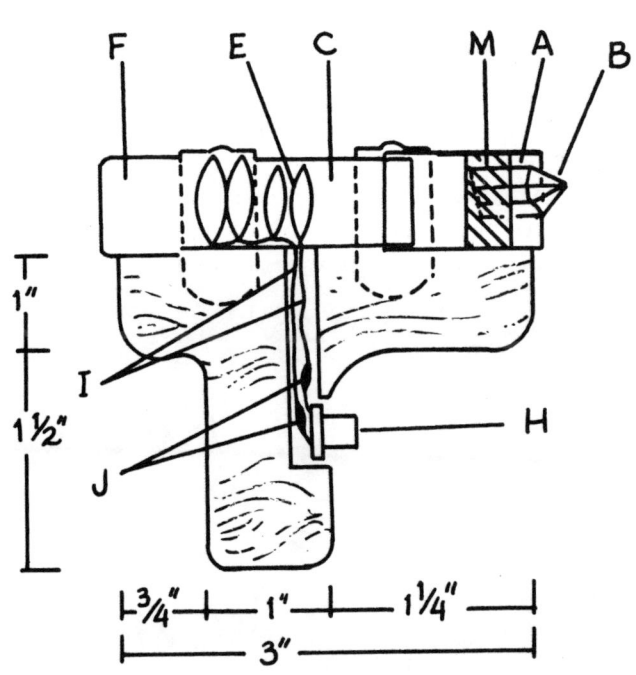

INTERIOR VIEW

CRYSTAL AMPLIFIER FOR MINI AEM

This amplifier adds length to the barrel of your mini AEM projector and also steps up its energy amplification with the addition of a second crystal. Since the amplifier is a separate unit from the mini AEM, it can be carried separately and assembled quickly for use without taking up the additional space in your pocket that a longer barrel would need.

Materials:

A. 1/2" diameter copper tube, 1-1/2" in length

B. 1/2" copper coupling to hold crystal

C. Quartz crystal, less than 1/2" in diameter, 1 to 1-1/2" in length

D. Copper foil tape or leather shim for crystal

E. Instant bonding glue

Construction:

The amplifier for the mini pocket pistol is built by attaching a 1/2" copper coupling (B) to a 1-1/2" length of copper tubing (A) with instant bonding glue. The quartz crystal (C) is mounted inside the coupling and glued securely. It can be pressure fitted using foil tape or leather as a shim if necessary.

This unit can then be slid in and out of the copper coupling around the crystal in the pistol barrel to extend the length of the barrel and amplify the power of the device.

CRYSTAL AMPLIFIER
FOR MINI AEM

CRYSTAL AMPLIFIER

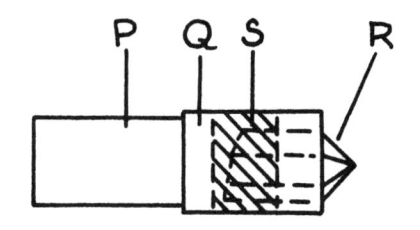

AEM MINI WITH AMPLIFIER

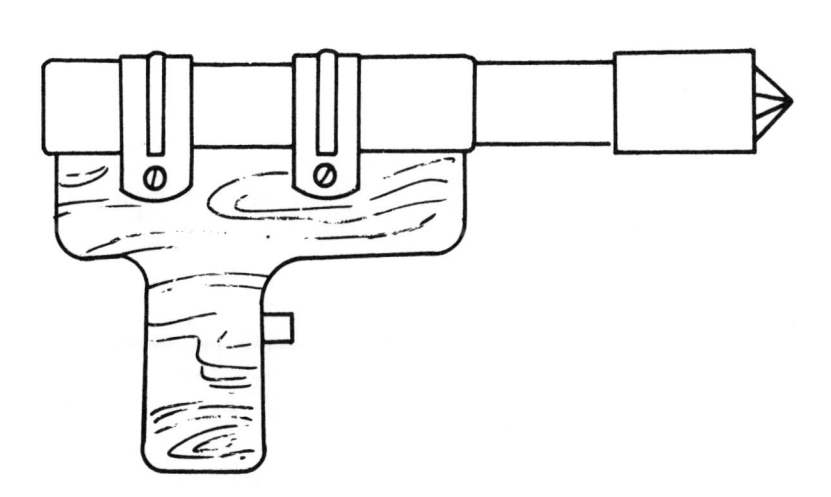

PART II

OTHER MAGICAL WEAPONS AND TOOLS

In this section we'll be discussing the making and use of magical weapons and tools, other than the autoelectromag. We define a magical weapon or tool as one that allows us to expand our known abilities in an unknown manner.

Magic has been around since the first cave man noticed that it rarely rained unless the sky was cloudy. Suddenly, he was able to forecast rain with a fair amount of accuracy. Chances are he became the clan's first shaman because of his magical knowledge. What he had in reality was a greater awareness of the Earth's natural rhythms.

Or, perhaps our cave man threw bones and predicted the weather according to the patterns they fell in. Were the bones really telling the cave man what the weather was going to do? Maybe. But isn't it more likely that our cave man was merely tuned into the natural rhythms and subtle shifts in air temperature and pressure that presage weather changes? In essence, that's what makes magicians—the ability to tune in and sense things that other people are unaware of.

Sometimes, in order to tune into these more subtle senses that we all possess, it's helpful to use tools. These tools give us a sense of confidence that allow us to perform feats that we wouldn't normally believe ourselves capable of. They allow us to bypass our conscious minds, that tell us something is impossible, and tune into the higher self that knows all things are possible.

Of course, many of the magical tools that we use may have a very sound scientific basis behind them. But, since we're not quite sure how to measure or quantify it, we classify the tool as magical. For instance, the authors are certain that the ability of crystals to amplify mental energy will someday be scientifically proven. Until then, though, crystals will have to remain in the mystical, magical realm. And that's not so bad. We all need a little magic in our lives to promote the childlike wonder that made life so fascinating when we were young. How boring life would be if everything was already known. The human mind always needs new frontiers to explore.

A common and popular magical tool is the athame, or a consecrated knife with magic symbols inscribed on the handle that is used for drawing magic circles. Any crystal knife can be turned into an athame by inscribing your own combination of magic symbols on the handle with pen and ink, a fine tipped marker, various colors of paint or even a wood burning tool, if the knife has a wooden handle.

Some practitioners attach a great deal of significance to using a new tool for each rite that is performed. This can get complicated and expensive. Our preference is to modify a high quality knife or dagger for continued use. However, if a "new" tool is desired frequently, there are a large number of knives and daggers in the inexpensive price range that are adequate for working magic. The same is not true if you require a new sword for every ritual. Even decorator swords are relatively expensive by most standards. A consideration of price also applies to any cup or chalice you may want to use in your magic practices. Copper, brass, silver and even gold-plated ones are inexpensive in second hand stores or at garage sales. These same cups can be expensive when sold new. Only you can decide which path to follow in the application of your magic.

Pentacles and magic circles used in magical rites can be outlined using various colored stones and quartz crystals, or just plain river rocks for that matter. Using your imagination and working with materials that you have on hand is part of the fun of magic. If you need more rocks and stones, a trip to the country is a good way to pick them up and have an enjoyable outing or picnic at the same time. To make things even easier, a magic circle can be outlined with chalk on a concrete patio or garage floor and erased after use.

Once again, one of the most important aspects of magic is the mind of the practitioner. Magic circles, tools, rituals and ceremonies are the outer form of magic. The mind, beliefs and visualization of the practitioner are the keys and catalysts that make it happen—the inner magic. The mind and spirit of the magician, witch, warlock or shaman are the ultimate force, not the tools they use.

BEGINNING CRYSTAL MAGIC

Magic is in the mind of the beholder. This explains why people just starting to learn about crystals and Earth magic can sometimes do as much, or more, than people who have been into it for a long time.

Choosing a crystal can give you the personal experience of establishing your private contact with the Earth. Pick up a quartz crystal. Hold it in your hand and feel the subtle energy. Try it with several crystals to feel the difference. Maybe you have several picked out that you like, but you're not sure which one to get. Hold each one in your hand until you find one that "feels" warm and comfortable to you. By this method, you'll know just which crystal is right for you. Your crystal is your contact with the Earth, which provides the materials for all our physical needs and wants. The crystal and you are children of the Earth.

What to do after you choose a crystal or a crystal chooses you? What do you want to do? If you know what you want, you can find ways to get it! A good place to start is with health. Good health and healing for yourself, your family, friends, pets and plants should give you plenty of material to work with.

To heal yourself, sit down in a peaceful place. Relax, and hold the crystal in either your right or left hand, whichever feels more comfortable. Close your eyes and see the crystal with your mind's eye. Imagine it pulsating with a blue-white aura of energy. Feel your own oval-shaped aura of energy around you. Then, visualize and feel the crystal's aura of energy growing and expanding until it encompasses your own energy field. The two auras or fields will augment each other as they reach a balance and the healing will take place. The reason this method of healing works is because nature's balance automatically provides the energy for health.

If you wish a spiritual balance of energy, or healing, for someone else, visualize the crystal's energy field engulfing them in blue-white light. The healing can be done with someone right next to you or even if the person is hundreds or thousands of miles away. The energy operates at any distance. This simple, natural, energy balancing is what we call magic because we don't know how it works—only that it does work.

Anyone who wants to, can understand and use universal or Earth energy. There are a number of ways to utilize a crystal to focus and send a healing balance, but they all draw on the same universal energy. The process we've just described is the same force of nature that keeps us alive, breathing and conscious every day.

Let's use a houseplant for the subject of a crystal healing. It could be a young plant that needs more energy for growth or an older plant that isn't doing well. Hold your crystal between your thumb and forefingers with its tip pointed at the plant from about a foot away. Visualize the crystal's pulsating blue-white aura and then imagine a beam of energy coming out of the tip towards the plant. Point the crystal at the dirt and sense the energy pouring into the plant's roots, coming up through the main stem all the way to the top of the plant. Talking to your plant lovingly, either aloud or silently, while you heal it enhances this healing process.

You've just completed a healing that many would consider shamanistic or magical. The same simple healing process can be applied to pets, people and the environment.

Healing is one of the most popular interests of people in our time. This stems from our natural desire to be in balance with the unity of all life. Being in balance is a natural instinct whether the practitioners are magicians, witches, warlocks, shamans, metaphysical healers or martial artists.

All magical activities require conscious awareness (not self-consciousness). A spontaneous smooth flow of life energy is the key. Everyone uses the same natural energy, but everyone should seek to find their own individual way of using it. Conscious awareness and unity with all life means you can relax and be yourself while performing magic.

The fact that you are the most important magical tool is nowhere more evident than in the practice of aikido or tai chi (*tai ji*). Here, the idea of natural energy flow and non-resistance to force, using the *ki* or *chi* energy, let us experience conscious awareness in action. This awareness can benefit us personally and be applied to everyday work and activities. The difference we spoke of before, between conscious awareness and self-consciousness, really shows up in a way we can experience for ourselves. The moves either work with natural spontaneity or they don't work at all. We would strongly recommend some practical knowledge and experience with aikido or tai chi for anyone who wants to learn about the magical uses of universal or life-force energies from Earth magic to shamanism. All of these areas of interest relate to the same natural balance of energy used in the martial arts.

Chapter 8

ANCIENT CRYSTAL WEAPONS

The past can be our present teacher.

Historical devices, remade into crystal tools, allow us to examine our human history, past lives, and inner selves on the path of spiritual growth. It's sometimes a good idea to look at where we came from in order to see more clearly where we are and where we and the human species are going. These crystal tools act as a focus that helps us recall our past history and past lives. The process is the mental and spiritual equivalent of time travel and can be not only informative and interesting, but fun. Our path of spiritual development hasn't always been straight and narrow, and we may have had some past lives that we have less enthusiasm for looking at than others. However, if we keep in mind that each lifetime provided us with valuable learning experiences that have brought us to our present level of development, then it's possible to take a dispassionate look at past traumas and marvel at how far we've traveled on our path back to the Source.

A MEMORY: THE OUTLANDS OF ATLANTIS

Technology without wisdom is like a lamp without a switch.

People of the other Earth continents had heard of the promised land of Atlantis. Small groups of primitive tribesmen from many other lands migrated to the fabled continent in boats and sailing ships, then settled in the forest lands of Atlantis and established their primitive communities. Gradually, Atlantean outcasts began to join these primitives, bringing crystals to the tribes.

The "magic rocks" fascinated the tribesmen and crystals were soon incorporated into their tools and lifestyles. Swords, spears, bows, knives and battle-axes appeared with the magic crystals attached to them. Even these small crystals had great power and religious significance for the outlanders, who could not imagine the cities, society, and crystal technology of far-away inner Atlantis. They were happy to acquire and use, in their primitive lifestyles, whatever power they could get and lived with the run-off of crystal technology that trickled down to them.

Most Atlanteans in inner Atlantis eventually lost touch with the Earth and nature even though they and their machines were duplicating nature's processes to a high degree. But Atlantean outcasts, rebels and ultra-sensitives joined with the nature-oriented tribesmen to form a new culture that used some modern technology and was still in attunement with the Earth. They had years to evolve into a breed of man suited for survival on Earth after Atlantis disappeared. Many of these men, rugged and easily able to adapt to the varied climates of Earth, migrated to continents in all directions before the downfall of Atlantis.

After Atlantis sank, these nature-oriented crystal users became the many tribes of Earth. There was a return to simple living as a reaction to the high technology that had destroyed the arrogant Atlantean elitists. In their search for a better way of life, the survivors assumed a humble attitude of reverence for the Earth and all life.

This attitude is attaining popularity once more in our modern culture, just in time to help us avoid repeating the mistakes of the Atlanteans. Our crystal tools frequently help us see the whole of our existence clearly; they help us to learn that the Earth and everything on it is interconnected and that to affect one part of the microcosm affects all parts.

RECALLING OUR PAST LIVES

After reading the preceding story of the past, you may want to find out about your own past lives. There are many ways to do this. Regressions, dreams, or memories that spontaneously arise are just a few of them. The least effective technique, although one of the most popular, is to have someone else tell you about them. Remember, that the information coming through another person may be accurate, but it's being filtered through someone else's consciousness. As with all spiritual development, the do-it-yourself path is always the best to follow.

One very effective technique for recalling past lives involves using a crystal tool and automatic writing. We've all had lifetimes that are particularly relevant to the one we are now living and they are the easiest to access using this method.

Seat yourself comfortably with paper and pen. Take a crystal tool from this chapter, or any crystal tool you choose, in the hand that you don't write with and relax a few moments to still your mind. Then write on the paper, "Tell me about a past life I have lived," or if you have a specific lifetime in mind that you want to find out about, ask about that. Next, all you have to do is write down the first thing that comes to mind, even if you feel a bit silly doing it. Don't worry about whether what you're writing is something that really happened or just something you imagination is conjuring up. It short-circuits the process and it doesn't really matter anyway, since what you write is bound to be relevant to you in either case. Sometimes it may take a few more written questions until you're relaxed enough to feel comfortable, but if you persist the process will work. Often, after you've received the basic outline of a past life, other questions will arise and you can write down those questions and the answers until you have as many details as you want. It may get uncomfortable to continue holding the crystal tool while you're writing, so feel free to lay the tool down nearby. Once you've jump-started the process, it will continue of its own volition.

One concern that people often express, when dealing with past lives, is that they may find out something so traumatic that they won't be able to bear hearing about it. To our knowledge, that's never been the case. Our minds just don't tell us something unless we can handle it. It's a built-in protective device. Also, keep in mind that we've all been murderers, liars and thieves in some of our past lives, as well as healers, magicians and priests. It's just part of the process of growth everyone goes through. What we did in the past has helped us learn and grow so that we have no need to repeat those experiences, and finding out about them can be both interesting and fun. Enjoy your past lives as you would a good movie or book, and learn from them when you can. But remember, this is the lifetime that really counts. It's up to us to make this life the best we've had yet by living every moment to the fullest.

CRYSTAL BLADE ROD

The crystal blade rod combines the ancient technology of the two-edged knife with modern space age plastic to create a perfect blending of new and old. It's somewhat more complex to build than many of the crystal rods, but isn't much more expensive. Larger in diameter than most other rods (1" in diameter), and quite a bit heavier, the length can vary according to the length of the crystal used (from 9-1/2" to 12" for the complete rod). Enclosing the blade is a copper cylinder that makes the crystal blade rod look like just another power rod to the casual eye.

The space age plastic blade has sometimes been called a CIA letter opener, despite the fact that it's strong enough to be driven through a wooden two-by-four. With the blade uncovered, the rod looks like a self-defense weapon, but like other crystal rods, it is first and foremost a spiritual healing energy rod.

The crystal blade rod has many practical uses. Outdoors, it can be stuck in the ground to provide a central focus of energy for a healing or prayer circle. Or, to provide an energy field for growing plants, stick four of the rods in the ground, one on each side of a garden area.

Another use for crystal blade rods requires two (one for each hand) for use in working energy while practicing spiritual development with martial arts techniques. Like wooden practice swords and bamboo wands, these can be used to extend and guide the *ki* or *chi* universal life energy. One should have some experience with the martial arts in order to take full advantage of these crystal energy tools in this manner.

Materials:

A. 1" copper end cap

B. 1" diameter copper pipe, 3-1/2" long

C. Two 1" copper couplings

D. 1" copper pipe, 2" long

E. Space age plastic knife, 6-3/4" long with nubs on knife handle filed off to fit inside 1" copper pipe

F. 1" copper pipe, 2-3/4" long

G. Copper mesh or foil tape wrapped around end of crystal and at base of knife to make them fit tightly in copper pipes

H. Quartz crystal, approximately 1" diameter by 2" length

I. 1" wide leather wrap

J. 1/2" wide leather wrap

K. Instant bonding glue

Construction:

The rod requires a 1" diameter copper end cap (A) fitted and glued with instant bonding glue onto a 3-1/2" length of 1" diameter copper tubing (B). A 1" diameter copper coupling (C) is then glued onto the other end of the copper tube. This makes the bottom handgrip of the blade rod when it is assembled and forms the cover for the blade.

The top section (crystal and blade) is constructed with a 2-3/4" section of 1" diameter copper tubing (F). The quartz crystal (H) is mounted in one end of this section using copper foil tape or copper mesh (G) as a shim and gluing it and the crystal (H) in securely with instant bonding glue. The crystal should be slightly less than 1" in diameter and 2" long or more.

The 2-3/4" length of 1" diameter copper tubing (F) has a 1" diameter copper coupling (C) glued onto the end after the crystal is mounted in the opposite end.

The space age plastic knife (E) (manufactured by A.G. Russell, Springdale, Arkansas) is available in most cutlery stores. The bulges at the hand guard may need to be filed or ground down so it will fit in the 2" length of 1" diameter copper tubing (D). The top 2" of the knife handle are wrapped with copper mesh or copper foil tape (G) as a shim. This is glued in with instant bonding glue. This 2" section with blade mounted is inserted handle first into copper coupling (C) on the crystal section of the rod and glued securely. About 3/4" of the tubing is inserted into the copper coupling, leaving 1-1/4" of the tubing (D) exposed outside the coupling. This exposed section forms the take-apart joint that slides into the copper coupling on the end of the lower handgrip section. Do not glue this joint in the rod. It's a good idea to put together the pieces or sections of the rod first without gluing them in place. This is to make sure they fit properly and to allow any adjustments in length of sections before the final gluing with instant bonding glue.

Wrapping the Blade Rod

This rod, like many others, is wrapped with leather strips about 1" wide (I). These are adhered with instant bonding glue. Of course, other alternative materials such as plastic, cloth or vinyl can be used if you prefer not to use leather.

The bottom handgrip with cap is wrapped leaving the cap and half of the copper coupling uncovered. The top handgrip that has the crystal in it is wrapped all the way to the crystal but leaves half of the copper coupling on the other end uncovered. There will be approximately a 1/2" wide portion of the copper tubing exposed at the take-apart joint. A 1/2" strip of leather can be cut and glued on this area (J) (see diagram).

This completes the crystal blade rod. We hope you enjoy experimenting and expanding your spirituality with this multi-purpose crystal tool.

CRYSTAL BLADE ROD

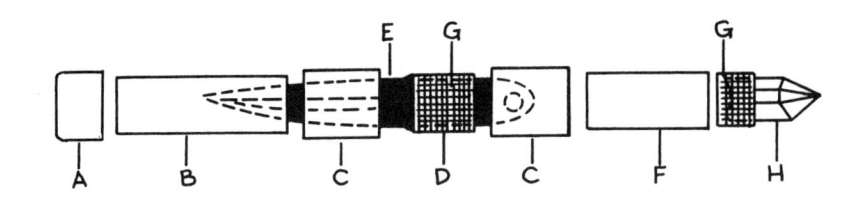

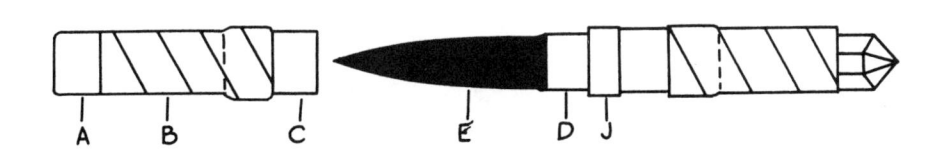

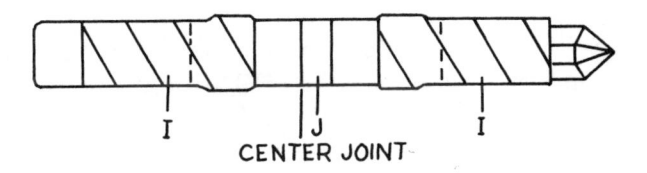

CENTER JOINT

CRYSTAL BATTLE-AXE

This crystal tool is one of the easiest to construct, and perhaps while you're using, it you'll remember wielding a similar artifact in a previous lifetime.

Materials:

A. 3/4" copper tubing, 4-1/2" length

B. 3/4" copper coupler

C. 2" long quartz crystal to fit 3/4" coupler

D. 3/4" wide leather strip

E. Stainless steel, uncovered battle-axe

F. Copper mesh or leather shim for crystal

G. Instant bonding glue

Construction:

Various types of battle-axes are available at cutlery shops or from arms reproduction companies. We used a short stainless steel model that came with no covering on the handle (E). This allowed for a 4-1/2" long piece of 3/4" diameter copper tubing (A) to be fashioned into a crystal mount. A 1/2" wide slot is cut in the tubing to a length of 3-1/2". The slotted tubing is placed on the axe handle and the sides of the slot are flattened with a hammer. This mounting is secured to the handle by wrapping several feet of 3/4" wide leather (D) around the handle and tying it in place. The crystal (C) is wrapped with strips of copper mesh or leather (F) and secured in one end of a 3/4" copper coupling (B) with instant bonding glue. The mounted crystal is then glued onto the end of the copper tubing mount previously attached to the axe handle.

Ancient Crystal Weapons

CRYSTAL BATTLE-AXE

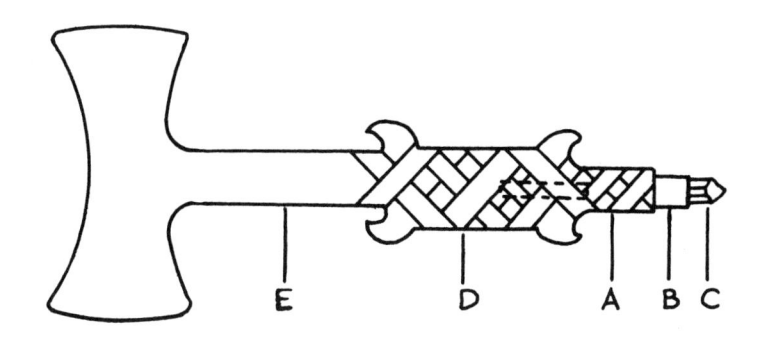

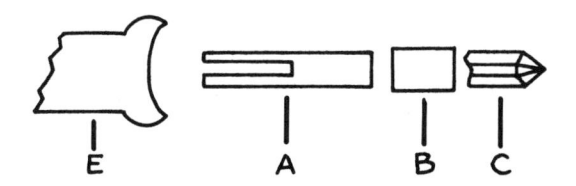

CRYSTAL WAR CLUB

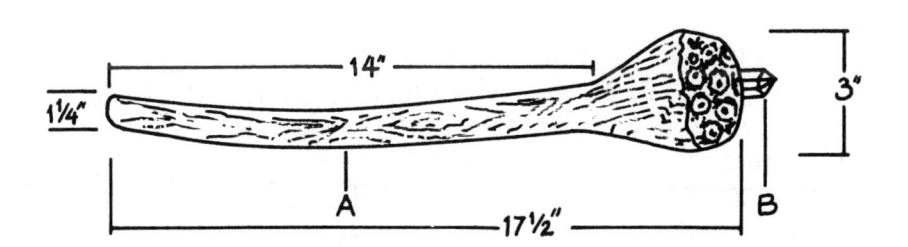

CRYSTAL WAR CLUB

The crystal war club combines the beauty of natural wood with quartz crystal. It's also one of the easier crystal devices to build if you can find a wooden war club that's already carved. If you can't find one, a club can be fashioned from any kind of wood you prefer.

Materials:

A. Wooden war club 17-1/2" long with a handle 1-1/4" in diameter and the bulbous end 3" in diameter

B. 2" long quartz crystal, 3/4" in diameter

C. Instant bonding glue or epoxy

Construction:

The club used for this project came from Polynesia, so if you aren't planning a trip there in the near future or can't find a reasonable facsimile, you might want to carve your own from a tree limb or shape one with power tools and a block of wood. Once the club is shaped to the dimensions given or to the size dictated by your wood, drill a hole 3/4" in diameter and 1/2" deep in the larger end. Then glue your crystal directly in the hole with instant bonding glue or epoxy. The club can then be stained or finished if necessary. This artifact, too, may bring back past memories or can be used in spiritual work to create new ones.

CRYSTAL SCEPTER

This is one of the more exotic variations of the crystal rods. The style and design make it ideal for ritual ceremony and healing. It's symbolic of human beings coming into balance and harmony with their higher selves. The crystal scepter is unique, with its beautiful cluster of quartz crystals that point in all directions while being connected to each other. It's a powerful energy tool that shows us we are all part of and connected to the one Source of energy. We promote the loving and caring for all life and all creation by building and using crystal energy tools like this one.

Materials:

A. 1" diameter copper cap

B. 1" diameter copper tubing, 8-1/4" long

C. 1" diameter copper coupling

D. 1" diameter copper tubing, 2" long

E. Copper reducer, 1" to 3/4" diameter

F. 3/4" copper tubing, 2" long

G. 3/4" copper coupling

H. Small holes drilled in copper coupling

I. Brass disc handguard, 2-1/2" diameter (from doorknob assembly)

J. 3/4" wide leather strip to cover handle

K. Quartz crystal cluster approximately 1-3/4" in diameter by 2-1/4" in height

L. Small gauge wire

M. Instant bonding glue

Construction:

The basic pattern starts out as a larger diameter crystal rod. The handgrip is assembled by using instant bonding glue to attach the copper cap (A) to one end of the copper tubing (B). The copper coupling (C) is then glued onto the opposite end of the tubing. The leather strip (J) is glued as it is spiral wrapped around the copper tubing (B) to cover the handgrip between the copper cap on one end and the copper coupling on the other end.

The 2" length of copper tubing (D) is glued into the end of the coupling (C). The reducer (E) should then be glued on this piece so that it fits tightly against the coupling. The 1" length of 3/4" diameter tubing (F) is inserted and glued into the 3/4" end of the reducer (E).

The Crystal Mount

This is the 3/4" copper coupling (G). At least a half a dozen small holes need to be drilled around this about 1/2" from the end (H). The coupling is then glued onto the copper tubing (F). Slide the brass disc (I) on the rod and glue it before the crystal is mounted. A gel type instant bonding glue can be used for attaching the disc, but a resin type glue like epoxy provides a more secure attachment when applied around the back where it meets the reducer.

The Crystal Cluster

The quartz crystal cluster we used has approximately 24 crystals of various shapes and sizes (K). A larger or smaller cluster can be used depending on your personal preference.

We used small gauge copper wire for attaching the cluster (L). This is done by running the wire through the holes in the end of the coupling and lacing it down across the cluster between the crystals. You may need to lace it back and forth several times at different angles for a secure attachment. Either brass or copper wire can be used, depending on the color combination you want. Brass wire will match the brass disc handguard and copper wire will match the copper parts. Or, if you want a different look altogether, use tinned copper wire or silver wire.

Nothing compares to the crystal scepter for spiritual work and recognizing your connection to the Source. It's even possible that you'll remember using a similar tool during the Atlantean era.

Ancient Crystal Weapons

CRYSTAL SCEPTER

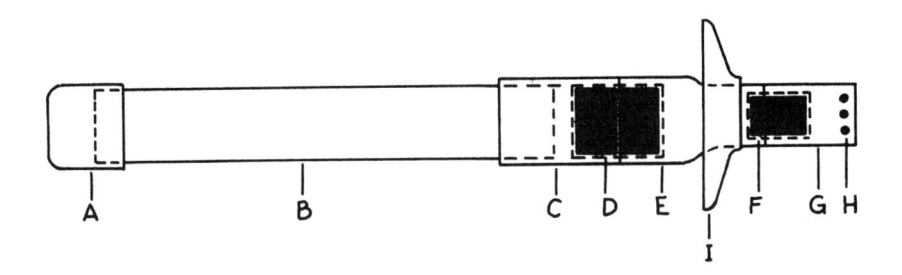

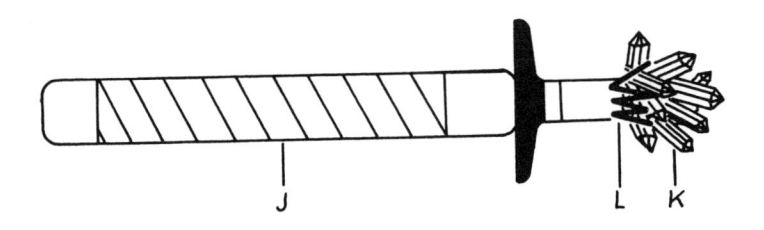

Chapter 9

CRYSTAL SWORDS AND DAGGER

*The sword of knowledge still carves
after the sword of steel is dust.*

In ancient times wooden swords, about forty inches long and deadly as steel, were used. Times have changed so that swords and daggers are now tools of spiritual development and practice. They are used to work with and expand the sphere of universal energy that flows through us naturally and forms our moving aura. These tools can also be used to project a beam of energy from our hands along the blade and outward from the point. Visualization helps start this process. Aura expansion and energy beam projection with visualization is done the same way as with wooden swords. Being one with the energy and sword or dagger, with no interrupting thoughts, occurs as a natural outcome of practice.

An understanding of some martial arts forms can be of benefit here, as several forms of martial arts use wooden swords of one kind or another. These swords are used to extend the *ki* or *chi* energy of the practitioner. This energy can be expanded to a larger sphere through the addition of quartz crystals. The short sword and dagger can be used to direct energy for circles, ceremonies and various magical rituals. Three different sizes of crystal swords are described here.

FULL SIZE CRYSTAL SWORDS

The wooden practice sword is approximately forty inches long and makes a perfect crystal tool for magic or ritual, or martial arts. It's available at most import, cutlery and martial arts stores. The sword is solid wood with a plastic handguard held in place by a rubber expansion ring. A brass or copper disc can be fitted between the plastic handguard and the expansion ring to dress it up. A metal sword of the same length can also be used.

Materials:

Wooden Practice Sword with Large Crystal Mount

- A. Wooden practice sword, 40" length (standard size)
- B. Brass or copper disc handguard (optional) 2" to 3" diameter
- C. Quartz crystal, 1" diameter, 5" long
- D. Copper pipe, 1-1/4" diameter, 5-1/2" long with two 4" long slots cut 1/2" wide (see diagram)
- E. Leather strip, 3/4" wide, long enough to wrap crystal mount

Metal Sword with Smaller Crystal Mount

- A. Metal sword, approximately 40" long
- B. Quartz crystal, 3/4" diameter, 2" long
- C. Copper reducer, 1-1/4" to 3/4" diameter
- D. Copper pipe, 1-1/4" diameter, 4" long with two 3" long slots cut 1/2" wide
- E. Leather strip, 3/4" wide, long enough to wrap entire sword handle

Construction:

The Crystal Attachment

The copper crystal mount is made from a piece of 1-1/4" diameter copper pipe about 5-1/2" in length. The copper pipe has two slots cut in it with tin snips. The lengthwise slots are cut 1/2" wide and about 4" long, directly across from each other (see diagram). The edges can be filed to remove the metal burrs and sharpness or the slotted area can be wrapped with one layer of vinyl electrical tape. This keeps the crystal mount from scratching the sword handle when it slides on or off. Two ways of attaching the crystal and crystal mounting are used, one temporary and one permanent. Even if a permanent mounting is desired, the temporary mounting is recommended first to check the balance and "feel" of the sword and crystal.

Temporary Crystal Mounting

This one is the easiest to attach and in most cases it is more than adequate for sword and energy practice. The sides of the slotted copper mount may need to be bent to an oval shape to match the sword handle more closely. The mounting will slide on, leaving the 1-1/2" unslotted end sticking out beyond the end of the sword handle.

The crystal can be up to five inches long, but it should be large enough in diameter to require very little material around it when it's fitted into the 1-1/4" diameter pipe or tubing.

If the crystal fits tightly into the end of the copper tubing, only a few short strips of leather are needed to press into the spaces between the flat sides of the crystal and the sides of the round copper tubing. If the crystal fits too loosely inside the copper tubing, a strip of leather can be cut to wrap around the base of the crystal so it can be twisted as it's tightly inserted into the tubing to form a pressure fit.

Then, long strips (1' to 3') of leather in a 3/4" width can be wrapped and overlapped tightly starting the spiral wrap around the crystal and wrapping downward until the crystal mounting is completely covered. The whole handgrip of the sword can be wrapped if desired. The leather strip can be tied or a leather thong wrapped around the loose end of the strip to hold it securely in place for the temporary mounting.

Optional Fittings for Copper Mounting

The larger mounting and crystal may be too heavy for some swords, either wooden or metal, so we devised a smaller crystal mount that can be used instead of the larger one. (This is the same type of mounting used on the diagram for the metal sword.) The balance can easily be changed by cutting the slotted end of the mounting shorter and by using a copper reducer on the crystal end to reduce the diameter from 1-1/4" to 3/4". This allows a much smaller diameter (3/4") and shorter crystal to be used. The mounting can be adjusted for size this way to radically alter the weight and balance of the crystal sword.

The mounting can be made even smaller and lighter by using 1" copper tubing for the slotted mount and a 1" to 1/2" copper reducer. This allows an even smaller (1/2") diameter crystal to be mounted. There are many variations possible and, fortunately, the copper fittings for each are readily available at your local hardware store, lumber yard or wherever copper plumbing supplies are sold.

For the simplest and lightest fitting of all, you can even pick a crystal that is approximately the same diameter as the sword and fairly flat at the base. Wrap the base of the crystal tightly in copper tape and continue wrapping the tape for about 1/2" up the handle of the sword, then continue wrapping back over the sword handle and base of the crystal again to be sure you get a snug fit. This fitting can be temporary or permanent depending on the amount of tape you use and how tightly you wrap it.

The Permanent Mounting

The permanent mounting uses the same copper slotted tubing and copper reducer (if necessary) as the temporary mounting. Use the permanent attachment after you are sure the weight and balance of the sword are right for you.

Wrap the base of the crystal with copper mesh or copper foil tape and glue it into the tubing or reducer with an instant bonding glue. Place the slotted section of the copper mounting on the sword handle and glue it with instant bonding glue. A leather strip (or alternative wrap) can then be started at the crystal and wrapped in a spiral as it is glued. The leather wrap can be used to cover the crystal mounting only or it can be be extended to cover the entire sword handgrip all the way to the hilt or handguard if you desire.

FULL SIZE CRYSTAL SWORDS

WOODEN SWORD

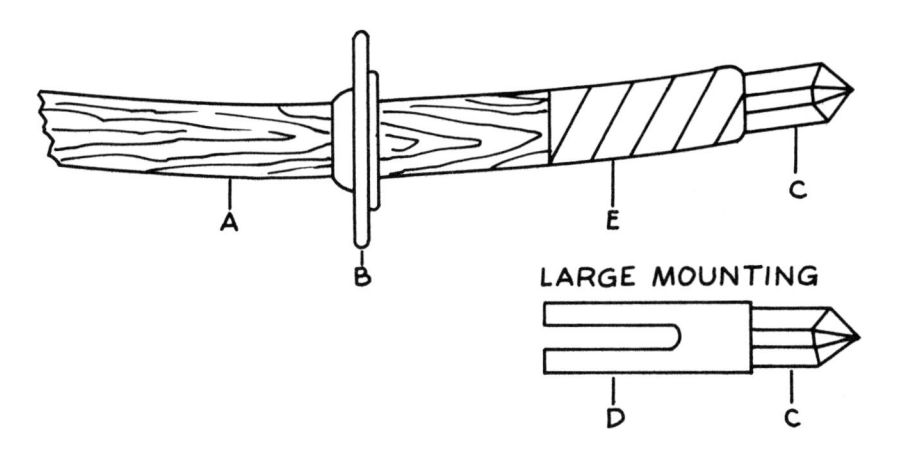

LARGE MOUNTING

METAL SWORD

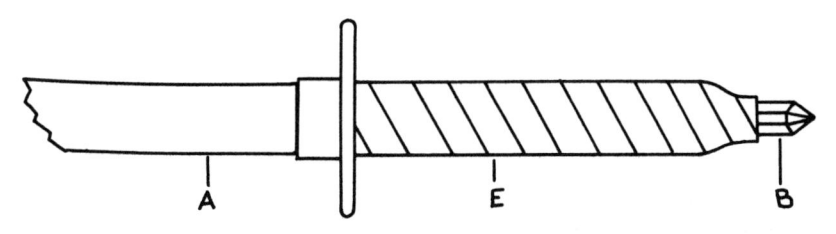

SMALL MOUNTING

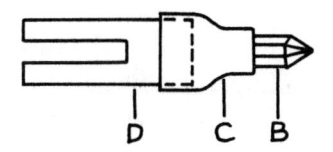

TWO CRYSTAL WOODEN SWORDS FROM ONE

One day we decided to buy a standard wooden sword (approximately 40" long) to create a new kind of crystal inlaid wooden sword. Naturally, we were excited and wanted to get the wooden sword right away.

We called several cutlery and import shops that usually carry wooden swords, but they were out of them completely and only ordered them once a year. We couldn't wait months to fulfill our vision and began to get frantic. Then we remembered another import shop where we'd seen wooden swords almost a year ago. They'd been hidden away in an obscure corner, so there were sure to be some left. We hopped in the car and drove across town to the store.

When we got there and looked where the swords used to be, they were gone. But we refused to give up and kept looking. Then we spotted it! The handle of one wooden sword sticking up in a tall basket of imported canes. We pulled it out of the basket with excitement.

At the sight of the full sword, disappointment set in. A wooden sword should have a close grain in the wood, no knots, and it should be perfectly straight. This one would have been perfect except for one deadly flaw. It had a knot about two-thirds of the way up the blade. This had caused the wood to warp after it dried. The last 14" of the blade wandered off to the right at an angle of over 20 degrees. Now we knew why the last sword was still there. It was useless for our masterpiece project, but we bought it anyway.

At home, we examined the sword and played with it for hours. It appeared there was no way that the sword would work. Then the answer came. We took it to the garage workshop, wrapped an old scrap of leather around the straight part of the blade so it wouldn't be damaged by the vise, then sawed the blade off at the base of the flawed angle. One bent sword became two straight ones. A little sanding put the tip back on the longer one (26" long). Some more sanding rounded and smoothed the end of the handgrip on the short sword (13-1/2" long).

We now had a perfectly matched set from the same piece of wood. The universe works in strange ways. We were now able to create two swords even more stunning than the one we had originally envisioned.

Materials:

A. Standard 40" wooden practice sword cut into a 26" length and a 13-1/2" length (1/2" of the 40" sword is lost from cutting, sanding and reshaping)

B. Quartz crystals for 26" sword—16 double terminated crystals approximately 3/4" long and 2 single terminated crystals 1-1/2" to 2" long

C. Quartz crystals for 13-1/2" sword—8 double terminated crystals 1/2" to 3/4" long and 2 single terminated crystals 1-1/2" to 2" long

D. Brass or copper disc, 2" to 2-1/2" diameter for handguard on longer sword (optional)

E. Leather strips 1/4" wide for wrapping handguards and ends of handles

F. Copper foil tape 1/4" wide for wrapping criss-cross pattern on handles

G. Clear epoxy resin glue for mounting crystals and covering each sword with final clear coating

Construction:

A 5/8" diameter hole needs to be drilled 1/2" deep in each end of each wooden sword. This is so a 1" to 2" single terminated crystal can be mounted in each of the holes just drilled. The crystals are not to be mounted yet, but they can be fitted, checked for depth and angle and then removed until later on in the project.

Handguards or Hilts

If a handguard or hilt is desired on one or both wooden swords, now is the time to cut and fit them. The handguard, as with the other wooden sword, can be a copper or brass disc 2" to 3" in diameter. Various pieces of copperware, brass door hardware, coins or almost anything made of copper or brass can be used for this. Most of these pieces can be found at garage sales or even in your own garage junk box. The center of the piece you select must be cut or drilled out so it slides over the tip of the sword down to where the sword handle meets the blade. This place is obvious on the larger sword, but on the small one, you'll have to pick a place for it about 4" to 6" from the butt of the handle.

After the handguards are fitted, take them off and lay them aside with the crystals for the ends.

NOTE: You may choose to omit the handguard on either or both of the swords. We put one on the larger one and left it off the smaller one.

Insetting Crystals on the Sides of the Blades

Now, the real work begins. Most wooden swords are slightly oval shape with a squared off top ridge line. It's the oval sides we're concerned with here or the center of the oval sides of the wooden blade, to be exact.

Make an indentation with a nail or pointed punch in the center of each side of the blade 1-1/2" from the tip of the blade. These are marks to show where to drill and cut out the 1/8" to 1/4" indentations for insetting the quartz crystals along each side of the blade. The other punch marks along the sides of the blade are 2" apart on center. There are seven more to make on each side of the blade on the larger sword, for a total of sixteen indentations (eight on each side). There are three more to make on each side of the smaller sword for a total of eight (four on each side).

Now, you have the marks for the center of each double terminated crystal to be inset horizontally into each side of the blade, lengthwise. The widest flat side of each crystal should be the side placed against the wooden blade (see diagram). Each crystal should be set, centered on the punched dot, where it's going to be inset. A pencil line should be drawn around each crystal. The crystals should be set aside in order, facing the same direction they were when the outlines were made. This can be done on one side of the blade at a time, or for both sides before the drilling, cutting and insetting is done.

A drill with a 1/4" drill bit can be used to start the indentation by drilling the center punched hole to a depth of 1/8" to 1/4". The hole drilled needs to be enlarged to the pencil outlined form of the crystal at this point. The sides of the indentation will be shallower in depth than the center. There are a number of tools you can use for shaping the indentations. A sharp knife and chisel will work, but a Dremel tool with a router-type bit is by far the fastest and easiest way to do it. You may also wish to experiment with other tools.

Make the indentations deep enough so that when the crystal sits in one, it leaves about 3/16" of the crystal sticking out above the wood surface.

It's better to do all the indentations for all the crystals on both sides of the wooden blade before mounting any of the crystals.

The handguards, if you choose to use them, must be put in place before the crystals are mounted since they will not slide on afterwards.

Mounting the Crystals

Clear epoxy glue is used to mount the crystals. Whether you use the quick kind or not, it should sit for several days to make sure the crystals are fully set in the deepest part of the indentations before any more work is done.

When the crystals and resin-type glue have set completely on one side, the other side can be done in the same manner. The side with the crystals already mounted should be laid on several thicknesses of soft cloth while the second side is worked on. This will protect the side that's already done.

Then, the two crystals set aside earlier, one for each end, can be glued in place after the crystals have been mounted on both sides of the wooden blades.

After the Crystals Are Mounted

The handgrips of each wooden sword (9-1/2" for the long one, 4-1/2" for the short one) are wrapped with two opposite spirals of 1/4" copper foil tape (available at stained glass supply stores). Each spiral is wrapped about a 1/2" apart so the handgrips are not completely covered except for a criss-cross pattern of copper over wood (see diagram).

The Final Resin Glue Coating

The crystals are mounted, the handguards (if used) are on, the handgrips are copper wrapped and we're ready to put several coats of clear resin glue (epoxy or other) over the whole thing—wood, crystals and copper wrap. A small brush, nail or stick can be used to spread this on after the resin and hardner are mixed together.

The swords can be covered with a light coat on one side at a time. Each side has to dry and set up completely before it can be turned over to do the other side. Light coats are recommended so that runs and bubbles can be avoided as much as possible. Each coat should be completely dry and set-up before the next coat is applied.

This part of the process can take up to three weeks because of the drying time between sides and coats of resin.

The Finishing Touch

The finishing touch requires 1/2" wide strips of leather or other material in any color you choose. The bottom end of the handgrip on the long sword is leather wrapped for 1-1/2". It's wrapped for 1" on the short sword.

The long sword is also wrapped for 1-1/2" behind the handguard and for 1" in front of the handguard. The short sword is wrapped 1" in front of the handguard. If handguards are not used, the area covered by leather wrapping is still the same in the same places. The wrapping can be held on with an instant bonding glue. Don't use the resin-type used on the rest of the swords.

The swords are finished. These are high energy crystal tools for any use. If the work is neatly done, they're also beautiful works of art worthy of display. You may want to buy or build a sword rack to hold the set. These are available at most cutlery shops. If you want a real thrill, there's nothing comparable to the feel and look of swords that you've created yourself.

Building your own tools of self-development and expression adds an energy you can't buy. It adds a vital part of yourself. These swords take time and work to build, but the energy and learning experience is one of those things that can't be transmitted in words or a book.

TWO CRYSTAL WOODEN SWORDS

TWENTY-SIX INCH SWORD

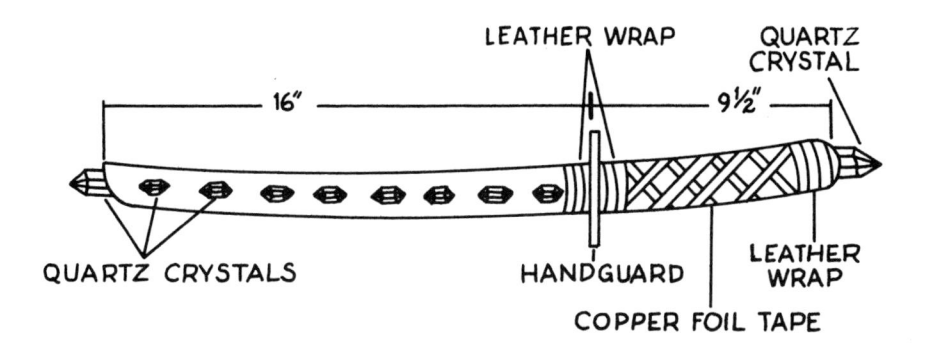

LEATHER WRAP
QUARTZ CRYSTAL
16"
9½"
QUARTZ CRYSTALS
HANDGUARD
LEATHER WRAP
COPPER FOIL TAPE

THIRTEEN AND ONE-HALF INCH SWORD

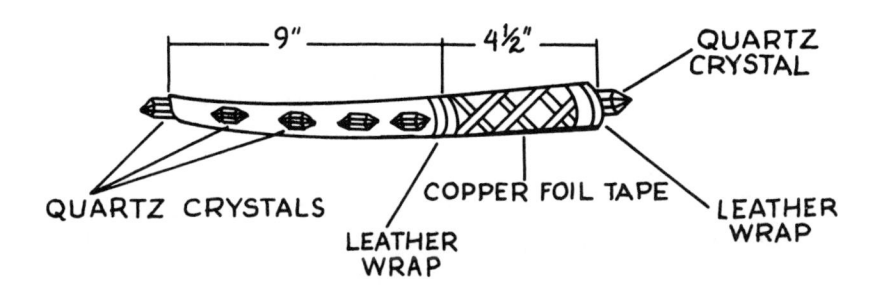

9"
4½"
QUARTZ CRYSTAL
QUARTZ CRYSTALS
COPPER FOIL TAPE
LEATHER WRAP
LEATHER WRAP

CRYSTAL EXCALIBUR SHORT SWORD

This example shows how the slotted crystal mount can be used on almost any kind or size of sword. The sword used was an excalibur decorative type with an overall length of 32"; the handle is 6" in length.

Materials:

A. Sword, 32" with 6" handle and 26" blade (decorator model is acceptable)

B. Quartz crystal, 3/4" diameter, 2" long

C. 3/4" copper tubing, 2-1/2" long with a 1/2" wide slot 1-1/2" long (see diagram)

D. Leather strip 1/2" to 3/4" wide, long enough to wrap entire sword handle

E. Instant bonding glue

Construction:

The crystal mount is a smaller version of the kind used on the wooden sword. This one uses a 2-1/2" length of 3/4" diameter copper tubing. The 1-1/2" long slot is still cut 1/2" wide. The crystal is mounted in the tubing with pieces of leather, copper mesh or copper tape for shims. Instant bonding glue is used to secure the 2" long quartz crystal. The crystal should be just slightly smaller in diameter than the 3/4" diameter copper tubing mount.

The crystal mounting and leather wrap (1/2" wide) can be put on in a temporary way with the tightly wrapped leather holding everything in place and tied tightly at the handgrip section near the handguard. A permanent mounting can be obtained by using instant bonding glue to attach both the crystal mount and the leather strip to the sword handle.

CRYSTAL DAGGER

There are many crystal knives in use today, but most of them are made by attaching crystals to some very fancy and expensive knives. What many of us need for everyday use is a crystal knife that looks good, is serviceable, and inexpensive. There are many small dagger-type and boot knives like this on the market for less than twelve dollars.

Ironically enough, one of our favorite daggers cost only three dollars. It was made in Pakistan, has a stainless steel blade, brass handguard, hardwood handle and a brass cap on the end. It's far better quality and nicer looking then one might expect for such a low price. It pays to look around carefully and examine what's available. It's also very simple to attach a quartz crystal to this type of knife.

Materials:

A. Small dagger or boot knife, 4" blade, 3-1/2" handle

B. Quartz crystal, 3/4" diameter by 1-1/2" long

C. 3/4" copper tubing, 1-3/4" long

D. 3/4" copper coupling

E. Leather strip, 1/2" to 3/4" wide, long enough to wrap crystal mount

F. Instant bonding glue

Construction:

A 1-1/2" quartz crystal is used. It should be small enough in diameter to be mounted inside a 3/4" copper coupling. This can be done by wrapping a 1/2" wide strip of copper mesh or copper foil tape around the base of the crystal and securing it with instant bonding glue.

A 1-3/4" long piece of 3/4" diameter copper tubing is used to attach the coupling with a crystal to the knife handle. One end of this tubing is hammered until it's almost oval and will slide onto the knife handle with a similar shape. Care must be taken not to bend the other end of the tubing. It must stay round so the coupling with the crystal can slide on and be glued. The oval-shaped end of the tubing is glued to the knife handle with instant bonding glue.

A 1/2" wide strip of leather wrap can be glued to the copper mounting as it's spiral wrapped. If the knife handle is wood, it looks nicer to only cover the copper, leaving the wooden part of the knife handle showing. If the knife handle is metal, you may want to wrap the whole handle to make it look better.

This crystal dagger is excellent for use in the practice of martial arts or can be stuck into the ground during a prayer circle. There are also a myriad of other uses, limited only by your imagination, for this crystal tool.

CRYSTAL EXCALIBUR SHORT SWORD

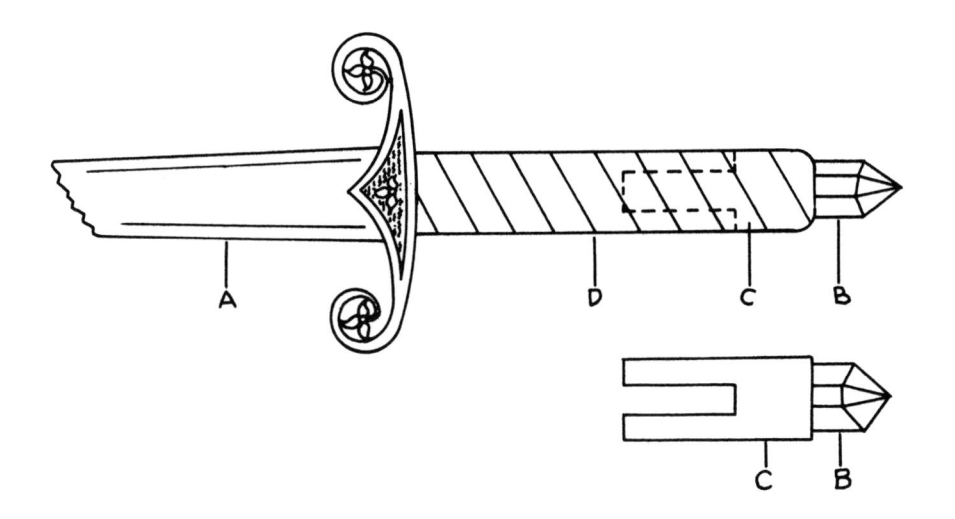

A D C B

CRYSTAL DAGGER

A E B

C D B

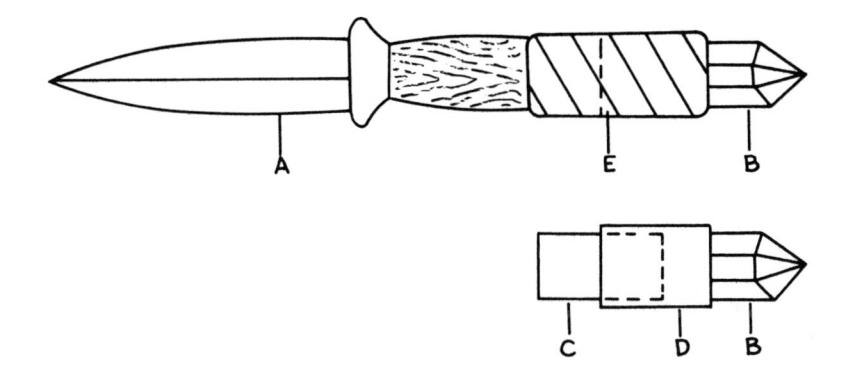

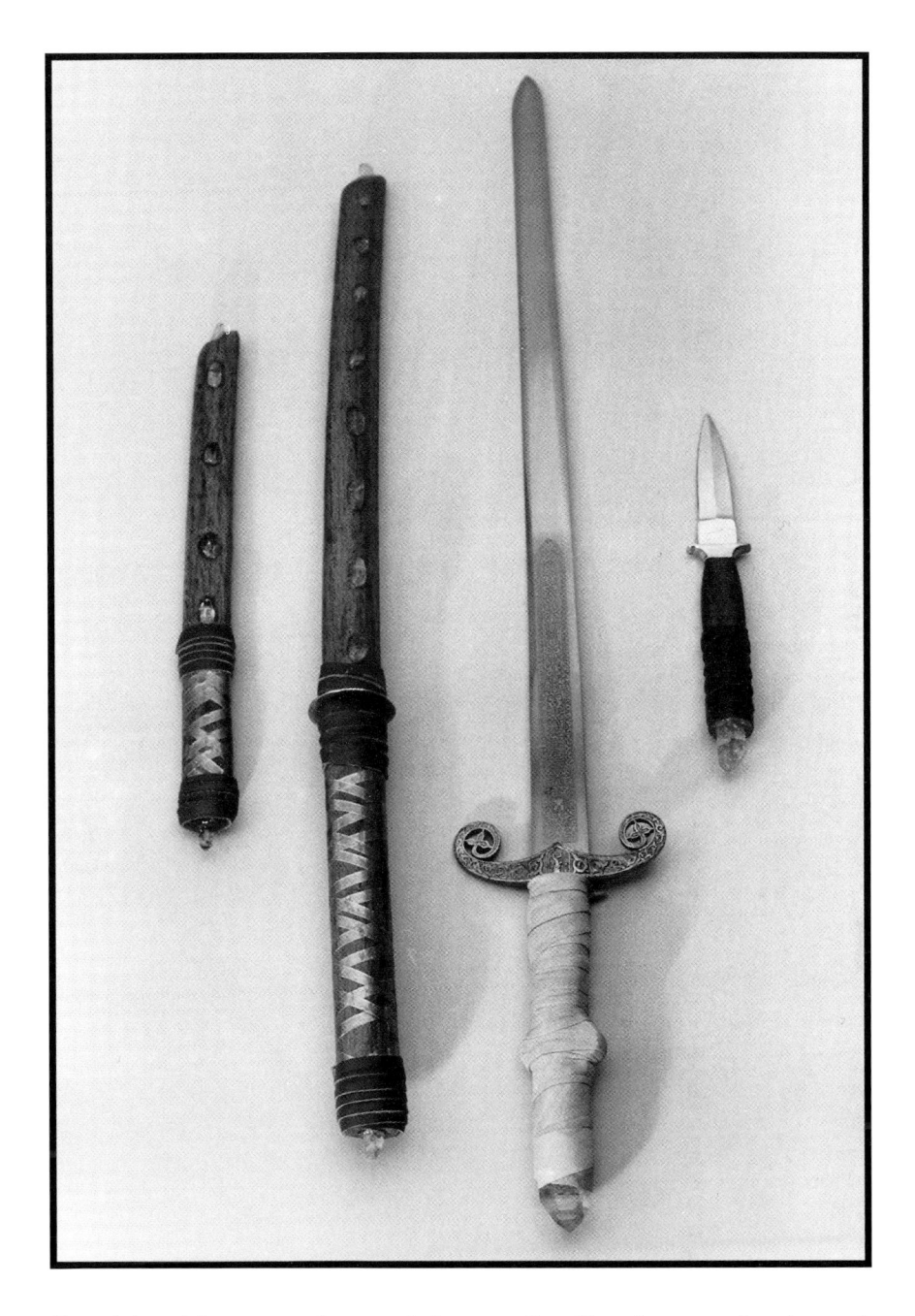

From left to right: two wooden swords from one, Excalibur short sword, and crystal dagger.

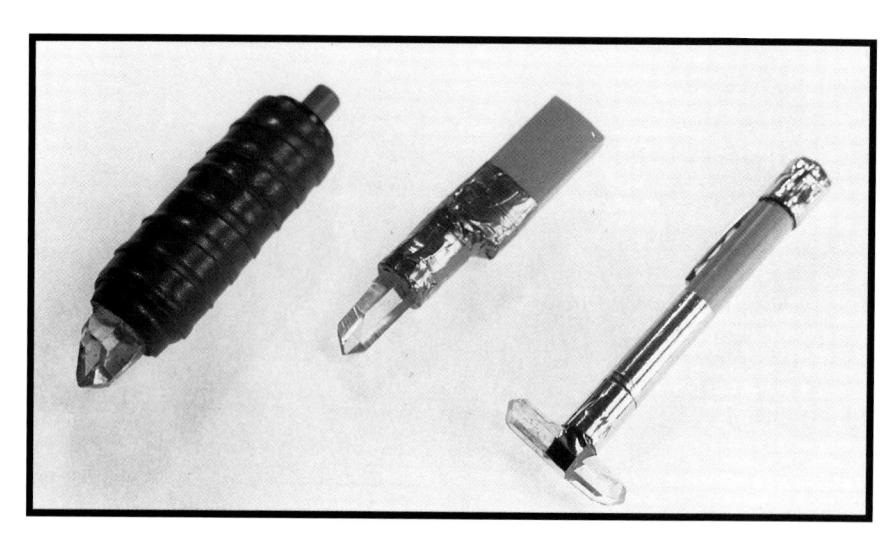

From left to right: piezo igniter crystal rod, squeezelight rod, and penlight rod.

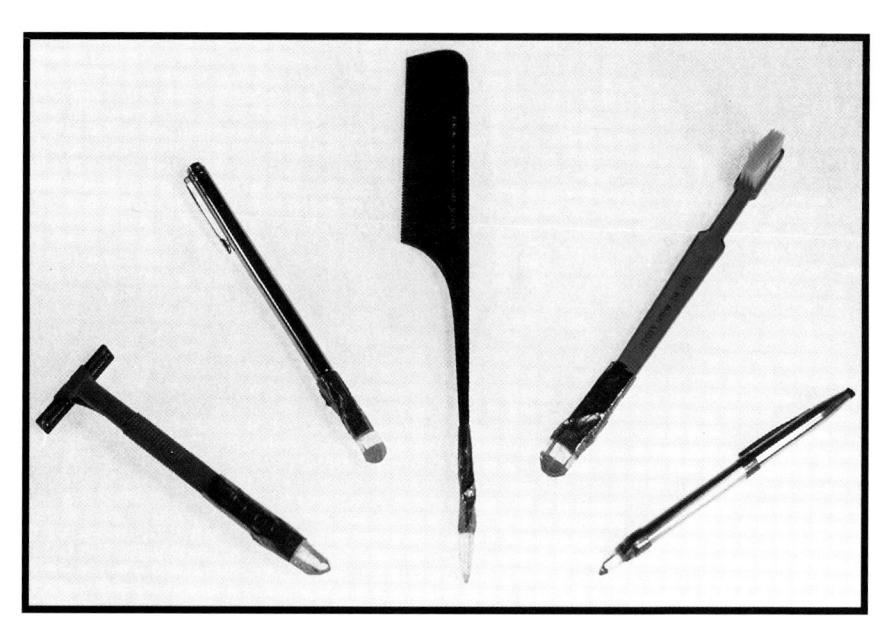

Crystal frivolities, from left to right: razor, pointer, comb, toothbrush, and pen.

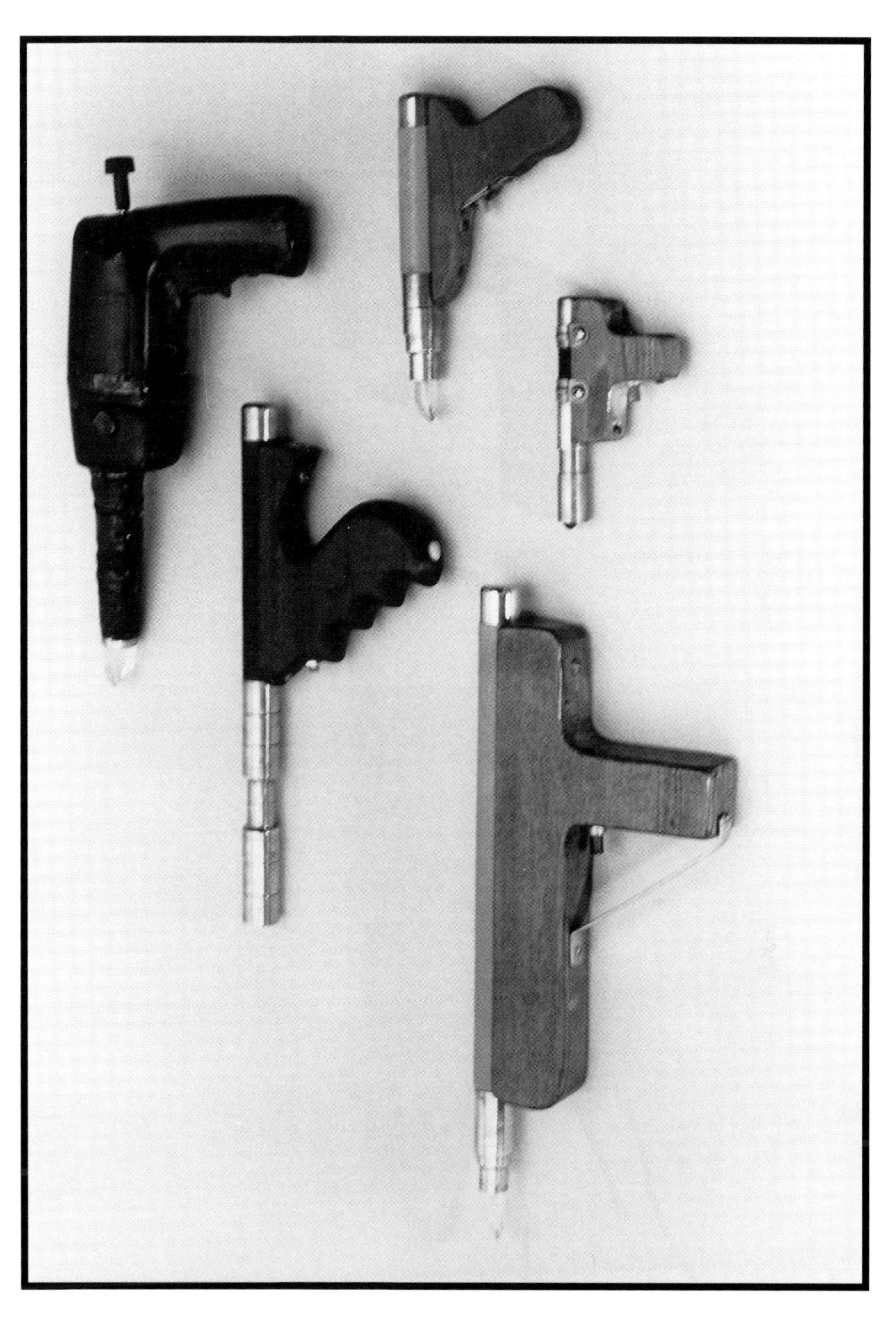

Clockwise, from top: psi-sub AEM, AEM beamer, mini AEM with amplifier, x-tal AEM, and space age AEM.

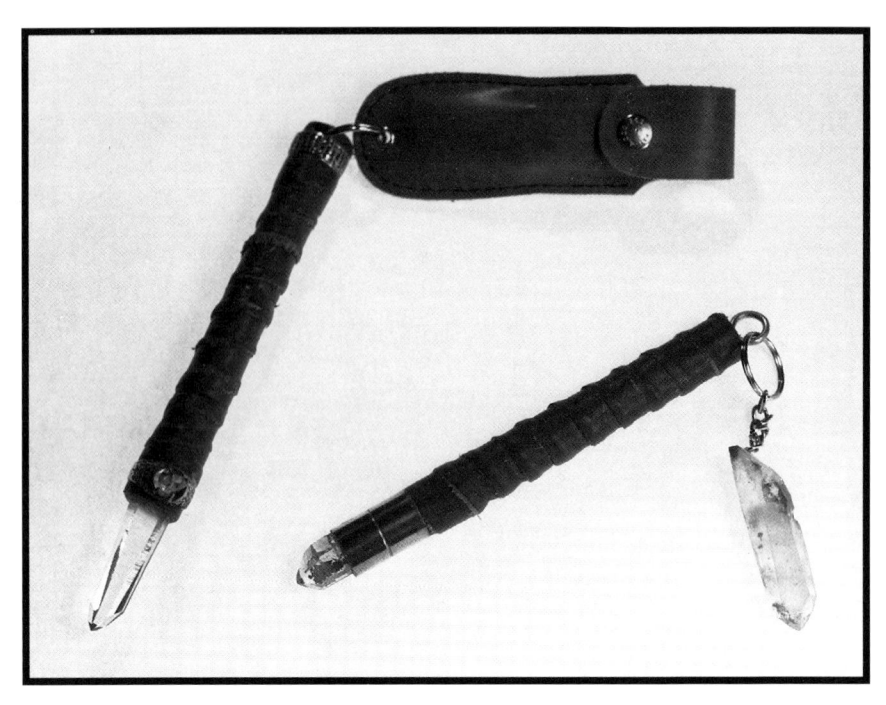

From left to right: special crystal defense stick and crystal self-defense stick.

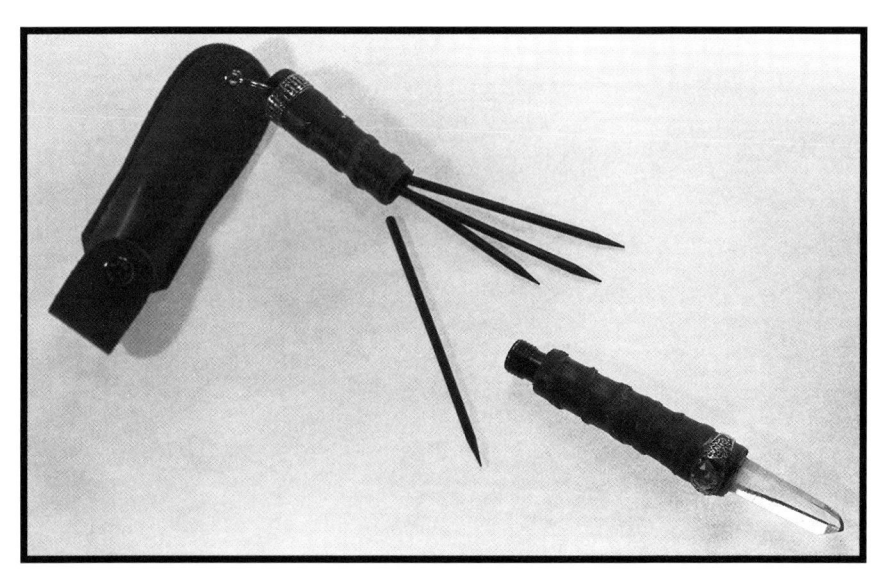

Special crystal defense stick.

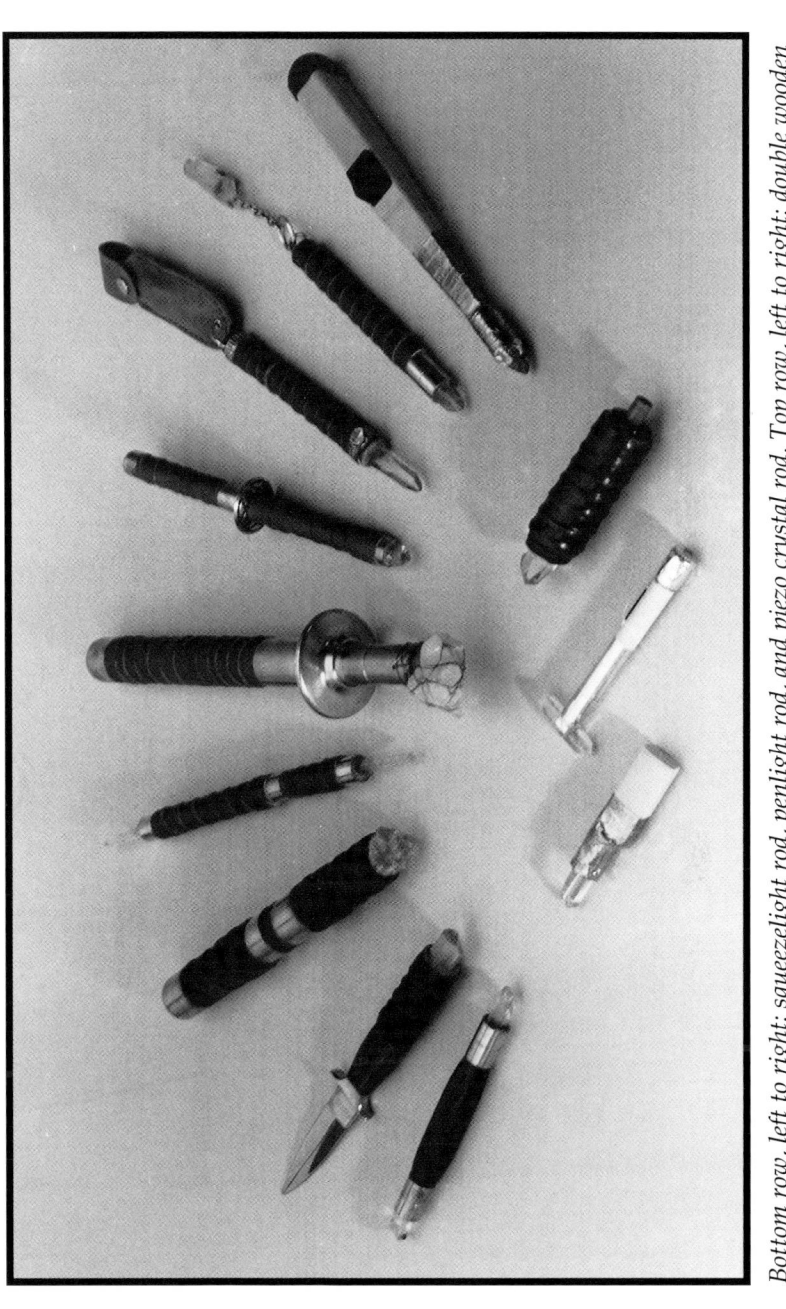

Bottom row, left to right: squeezelight rod, penlight rod, and piezo crystal rod. Top row, left to right: double wooden crystal rod, crystal dagger, crystal blade rod, triple crystal spike rod, crystal scepter, crystal container rod, two crystal self-defense sticks, and piezo crystal rod.

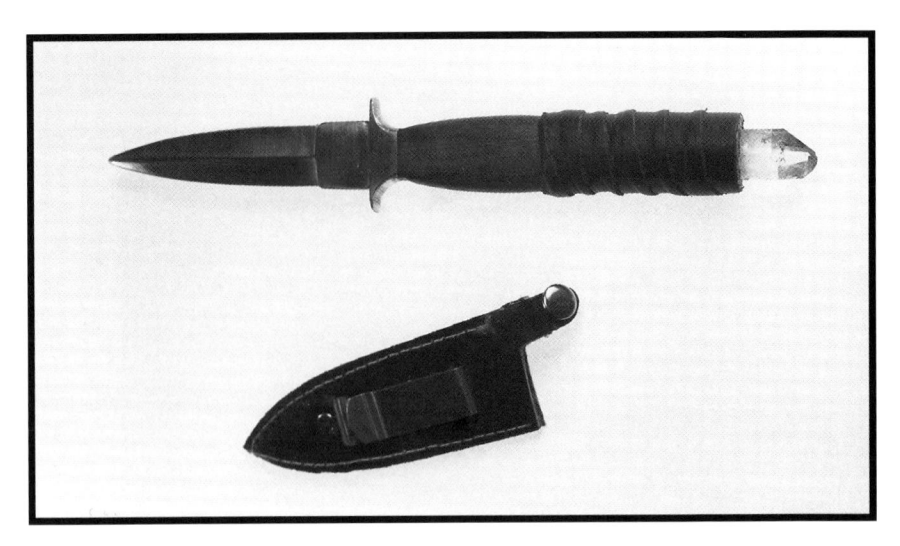

Crystal dagger and sheath.

Crystal blade rod.

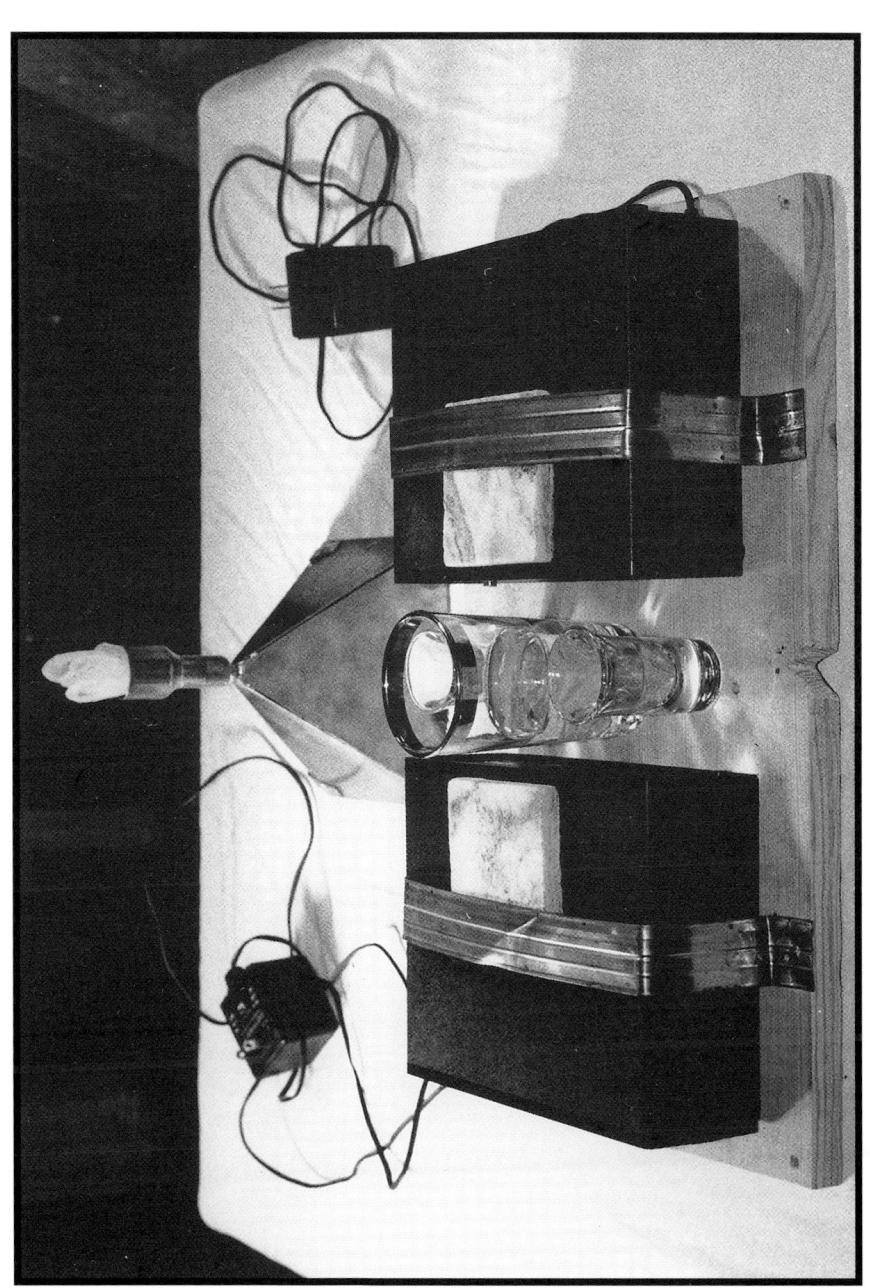

Crystal water (nion) generator.

Crystal scepter.

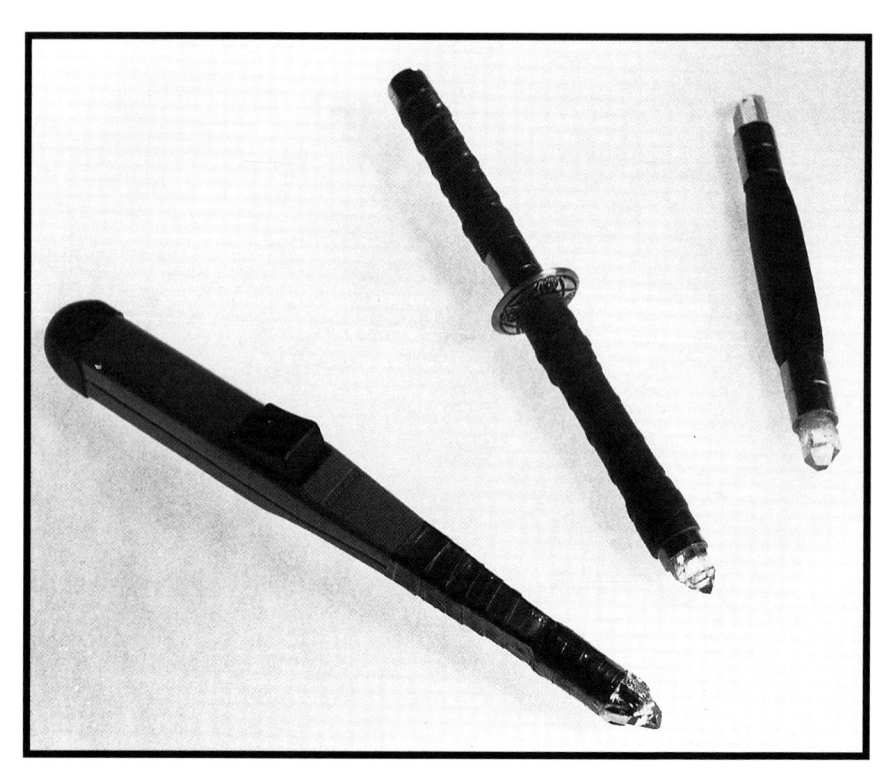

From left to right: piezo crystal rod, crystal container rod, and double wooden crystal rod.

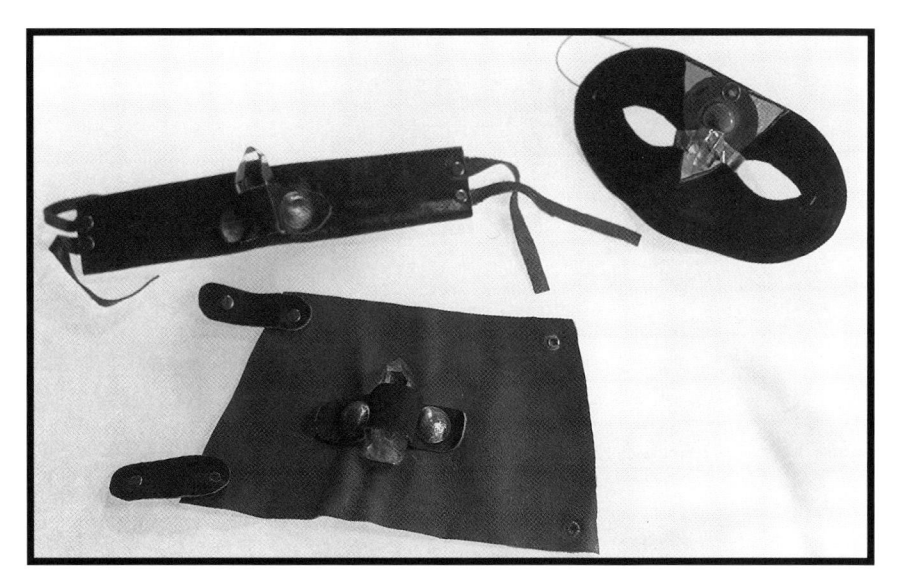

Clockwise, from top: crystal mask, warrior armband, and Amazon anklet.

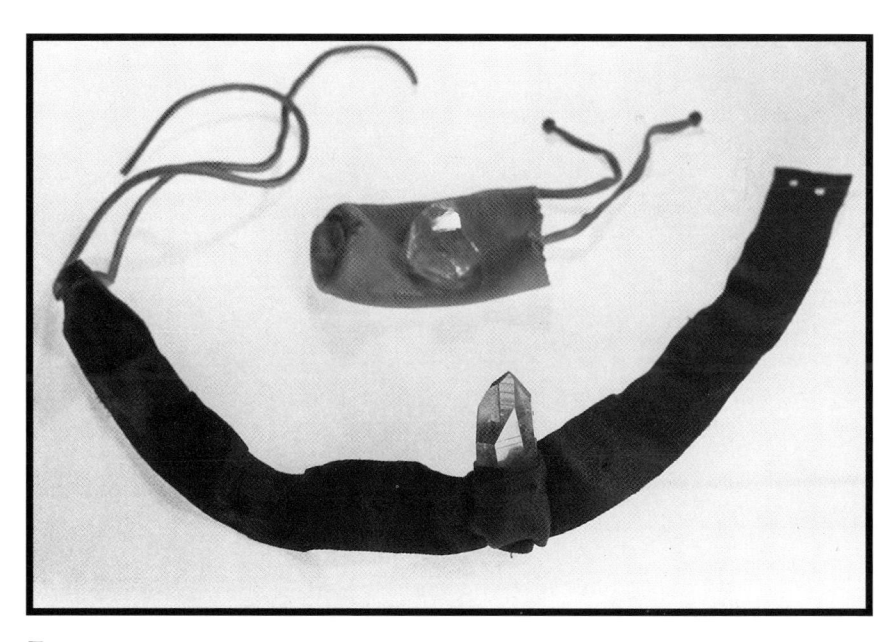

Top: aura amplifier. Bottom: aural headband.

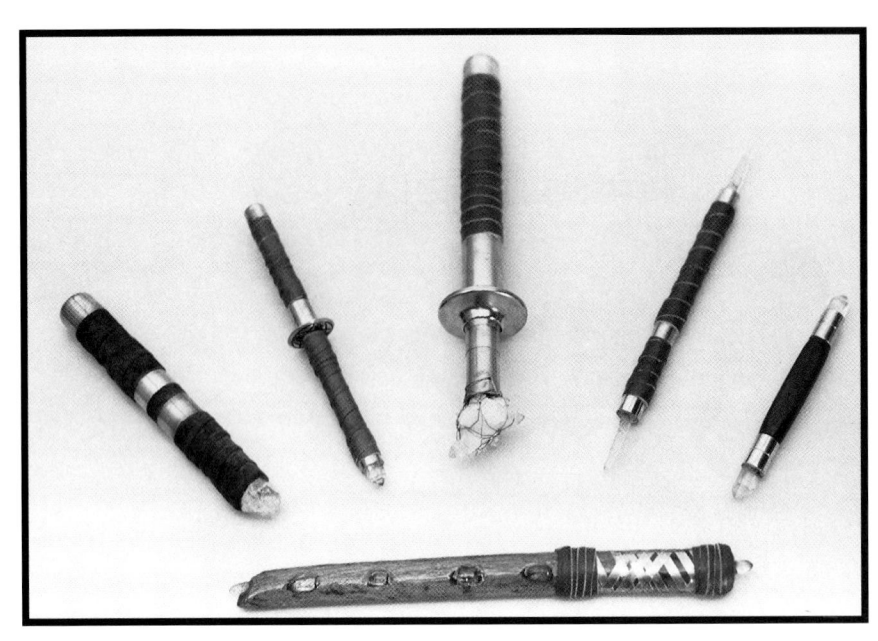

Top row, left to right: crystal blade rod, crystal container rod, crystal scepter, triple crystal spike rod, and double wooden crystal rod. Bottom: 13-1/2" crystal wooden sword.

Aura amplifiers in heatsink stands.

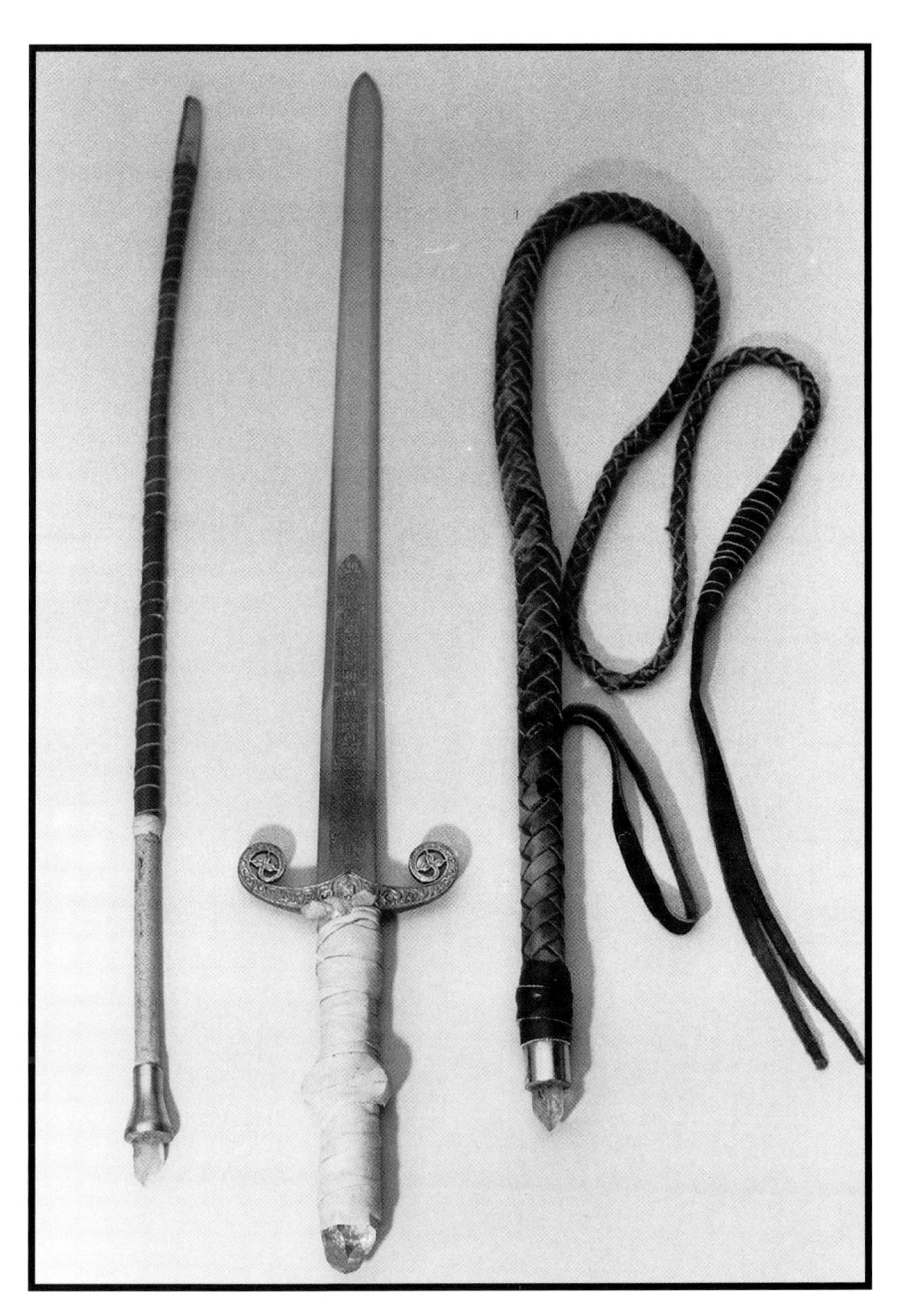

From left to right: crystal riding crop, Excalibur short sword, and crystal bullwhip.

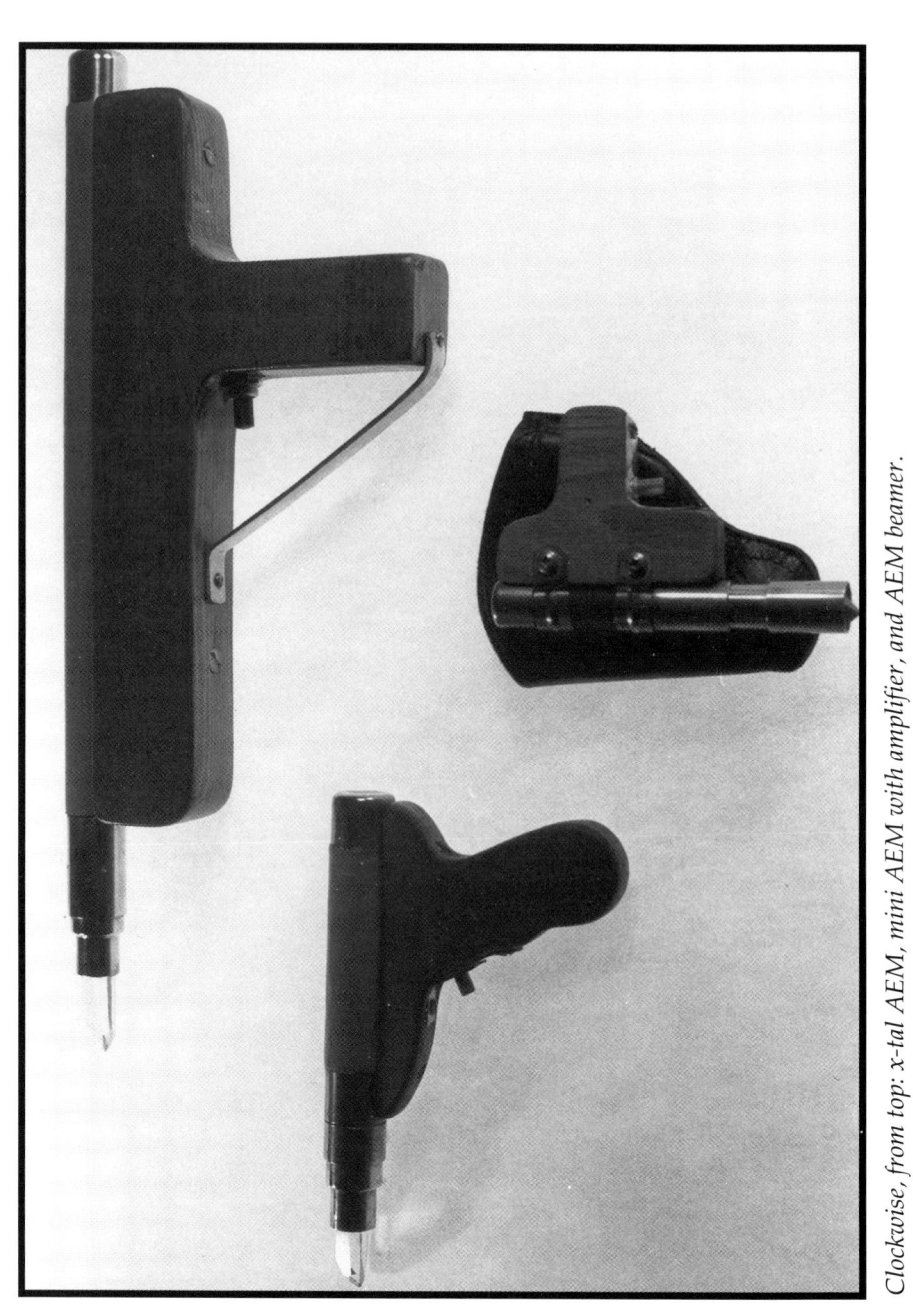

Clockwise, from top: x-tal AEM, mini AEM with amplifier, and AEM beamer.

Chapter 10

CRYSTAL SELF-DEFENSE STICKS

*If you have to defend yourself—
you're not in tune with yourself.*

It's been said the defense stick was originally invented by a Korean police chief to help women in his city defend themselves from attack. It's a practical invention as well, since it holds your ring of keys with a metal ring on the end of a 5 to 6" long stick. These rods are approximately a 1/2" in diameter and come in various forms of metal or hard plastic. Defense sticks are available at most cutlery shops or martial arts supply stores.

Materials:

All Models

- A. 1-1/2" to 2" long quartz crystal, slightly less than 1/2" diameter
- B. Copper mesh or copper foil tape, 1/2" wide for wrapping and mounting crystal
- C. Instant bonding glue

D. 1/2" copper coupling

E. Self-defense stick, standard 5-1/2" length in metal or plastic (the metal ring to hold a key chain is part of the standard unit)

F. Leather strip 1/2" wide, long enough to wrap stick (two strips for the special crystal defense stick)

G. Key ring knife or crystal on chain to use instead of keys on key ring (optional)

NOTE: Crystal mountings are the same since all models are the same size.

Construction:

The Quartz Crystal Mountings

The crystal mounting described here is the same for all self-defense sticks. Like many other rods, the base of the crystal is wrapped and glued with a strip of 1/4 to 1/2" wide copper mesh or copper foil tape. This acts as a shim so the base of the crystal can be fitted securely into a 1/2" copper coupling. The wrapping can be then be flattened so it's flush with the end of the coupling by using a flat screwdriver or knife blade. Soak the wrapping with instant bonding glue after the crystal is straightened. The base of the crystal should only occupy half of the coupling. The other half of the coupling should be open to fit on the end of the self-defense stick.

While all defense sticks are similar, two of the crystal types are very much alike. One is solid hard plastic and one is solid metal (probably aluminum). Both can be fitted with the crystal and copper coupling mount. Some need a bit of filing and rasping since they're slightly larger than the 1/2" diameter coupling. Other, smaller ones, may need a thicker wrapping around the end of the crystal to make them fit the coupling. The crystal in its coupling is then attached to the defense stick using an instant bonding glue.

Finishing Touches

At this point, you can leave it as it is, a black or silver defense stick with a copper coupling and crystal on the end. Your ring of keys can be put on the other end and you're ready with a complete unit to be used as a healing rod, key ring or for self-defense.

Or you can wrap the stick with a 1/2" wide strip of leather in the color of your choice. Instant bonding glue is applied to the stick as the leather is wrapped in a spiral pattern. The copper coupling crystal mount can be wrapped with leather or left exposed while the rest of the stick is wrapped, according to your preference.

Optional Wrapping Materials
Some people prefer not to use leather for wrapping their crystal rods. In these cases, there are quite a few other options. Various vinyl and/or cloth strips can be used as a wrapping. We even covered a crystal rod with denim material by cutting a strip 2 to 2-1/2" wide, then wrapping it around the rod and sewing it up the seam along one side with a needle and heavy thread. All kinds of tapes can be used to cover rods. And while some don't look quite as nice as leather, they all work energy the same way. Even heavy string or yarn have been glued and wrapped around crystal rods with successful results.

Decorations and Attachments
Since all the crystal self-defense sticks have a metal ring on one end, this allows one to choose from a wide variety of attachments or decorations. Naturally, a heavy ring with keys was intended to be part of this unit at first. However, crystal key chains with quartz or amethyst crystals may also be attached. They're nice looking as well as functional with a 2 to 2-1/2" stone. These work in more ways than one and aren't just a decoration. The crystal key chain on the end can also function as a pendulum for dowsing. The crystal key chain makes the stick the most versatile, but there are many other options available.

Anything that fits on a key ring will fit on the end of the stick. This includes key ring pocket knives and key ring flashlights. Even large silver or gold pendants, with or without gemstones, can be used on the key ring as decorations.

SPECIAL CRYSTAL DEFENSE STICK

There's another type of crystal defense stick that's more versatile than the others. It's a hollow metal stick about 5-1/4" in length, and it unscrews in the middle to allow access to an inner compartment in the tube.

This one is beautiful with a clear 2-1/2" quartz crystal mounted on one end. Leather can be wrapped on each of the two halves of the stick so that the place where they join is almost invisible. The key ring on the other end can have a 2 to 3" quartz crystal with a 2-1/2" chain and key ring.

Or you can attach a leather key ring pouch on the end of the crystal self-defense stick. The pouch usually contains mace, which is worthless for defense. Throw the mace away and keep the key ring leather pouch. You could put a crystal or one of the spring loaded collapsible martial arts throwing stars into the leather pouch. These stainless steel throwing stars are made in Japan and available in most cutlery or knife shops.

We mentioned this defense stick was hollow, but didn't mention that it comes with four 4" long steel darts, or spikes, inside. If the spikes don't appeal to you, you may want to use the space inside for money, spiritual diagrams, or important (small) papers.

All defense sticks can be enhanced by silver or gold bands or rings with gemstones if they are the right size to fit tightly over the wrapping on the stick. Don't glue these on unless you're sure you won't want to take them off for other uses. We, personally, prefer a silver band right at the key-ring end and a silver ring with a quartz crystal at the crystal mounting end.

SUGGESTED USES FOR CRYSTAL DEFENSE STICKS

Using the crystal self-defense sticks is like using any other crystal device. A few ways to use these tools are:

1. Use them in pairs, one in each hand. The slow movements of tai chi are especially adaptable to crystal tools. The slow motion movements allow people to see and feel what they are really doing, inside and out.

2. Dowsing with a crystal key chain on the end of a self-defense stick is another good way to use it.

3. Meditate with your crystal self-defense stick.

4. Use the self-defense stick for healing as you would a crystal rod. Hold the crystal end of the stick slightly above the area

to be healed and project the healing, white light energy through the crystal with your mind.

5. Carry the crystal self-defense stick in your hand when you're in a situation where there might be danger. As you hold it, project white light energy and love out the end of the stick and cause the light to surround you and the area nearby. Thus protected, you should never have to use the stick to physically protect yourself because those who are holding harmful thoughts or hate will either shun the area around you or find their own thoughts becoming more positive.

6. Crystal defense sticks are the perfect addition to magical or shamanic rituals and ceremonies.

Comments:

These uses and others all draw on the same universal life force energy used in the practice of many martial arts forms or healing and meditation practices. The energy in all the varied uses of crystal devices is not just related—it is one and the same. Whether for practicality, healing, dowsing, defense or just entertainment, these crystal defense stick projects will help you on your journey into the future.

CRYSTAL SELF-DEFENSE STICKS

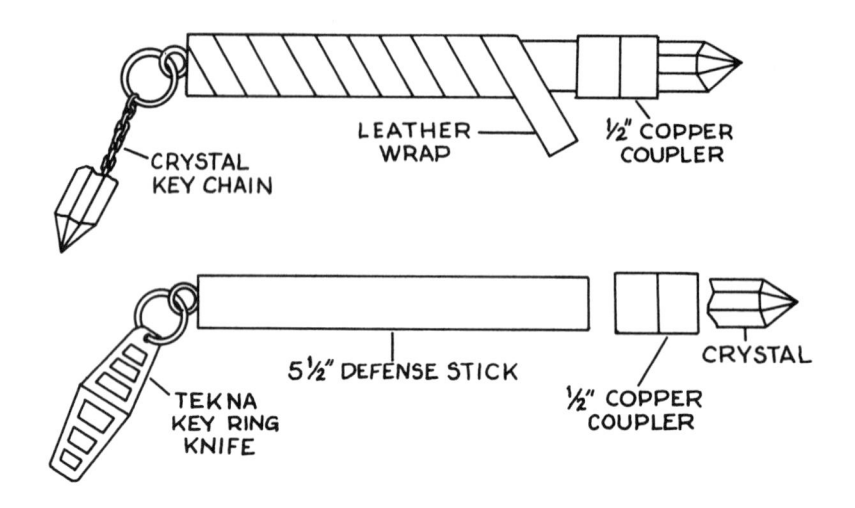

- CRYSTAL KEY CHAIN
- LEATHER WRAP
- ½" COPPER COUPLER
- TEKNA KEY RING KNIFE
- 5½" DEFENSE STICK
- ½" COPPER COUPLER
- CRYSTAL

SPECIAL CRYSTAL DEFENSE STICK

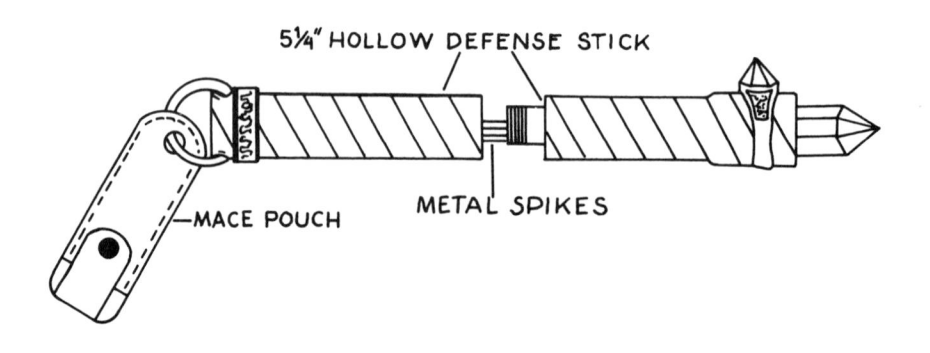

- 5¼" HOLLOW DEFENSE STICK
- MACE POUCH
- METAL SPIKES

Chapter 11

AURA AMPLIFIERS AND ACCESSORIES

Auras reflect the spiritual essence that our bodies hide.

AURA AMPLIFIERS

Each of us has an invisible aura of energy vibrating around us at all times. Carrying a crystal or having one nearby will intensify and amplify this aura while increasing the rate of its vibrations. The faster vibrations of our auras help us tune into a higher state of consciousness. Some people are more sensitive to the energy of crystals than others. If you haven't been around crystals before, you may find yourself feeling slightly nervous or jumpy in their presence at first. This can be unsettling, but it's a clear sign that you are raising your vibrational level to one that's much more aware and conscious. Also certain crystals may provoke this reaction more than others. If you do experience this phenomenon, don't worry, it will pass when your vibrational level has increased. To minimize this effect, try using a different crystal or you can clear your crystal of other energies it may have picked up and reprogram it.

Clearing the crystal is easy. All you need do is hold it in your hand and imagine pure white light energy flowing through it. It helps to augment this procedure with a feeling of unconditional love. Then, you can program it with positive thought and emotional energy while visualizing an aura of blue-white energy radiating from the crystal and forming an energy sphere around it.

Materials:

A. Your favorite crystal, a size convenient to carry

B. A small bag or pouch

C. A small stand

Construction:

The aura amplifier may be the easiest crystal tool to put together. All you really need is your favorite quartz crystal. The crystal should be one that you feel comfortable handling and carrying with you all the time. The size and shape of the crystal are determined by what is convenient for you to carry. Remember, this crystal will be in your pocket or purse almost all the time. The crystal might be as small as 1" long by 1/2" in diameter or as large as 3" long by 3/4" in diameter. These are approximate guidelines only. The one you choose to carry may be smaller or larger, depending on your personal preference.

The next item you'll need is a small bag for carrying the crystal. The bag can be made out of leather or cloth, and should have a drawstring or flap to close it. The bag will keep your crystal from getting damaged while it's in your pocket or purse, and will also keep the crystal from damaging anything else you are carrying with it.

Place the crystal in the bag and it will keep radiating its positive energy aura as you carry it with you throughout the day. You can also boost its effect by visualizing radiant universal life energy enhancing and amplifying the aura around you whenever you feel the need or desire.

When you're at home or at work, you may prefer to have the crystal out where you can see it. If this is the case, take the crystal out of its bag and place it on a holder or stand in a convenient place. Visualize the aura of energy expanding to encompass your whole house and property or place of business.

The stand for your crystal can be almost anything you choose.

A wooden stand or any kind of candle holder will work. Some of our favorite holders are copper pyramid or black diamond-shaped heat sinks (available at many electronic supply stores) that can be bent and formed to fit the crystal. There are also many other items that can be adapted for crystal stands. Use your imagination and choose something that you like for this purpose. The aura amplifier can add beauty and good energy to your days and can even benefit others around you who come into the sphere of your expanded aura.

AURA AMPLIFIER

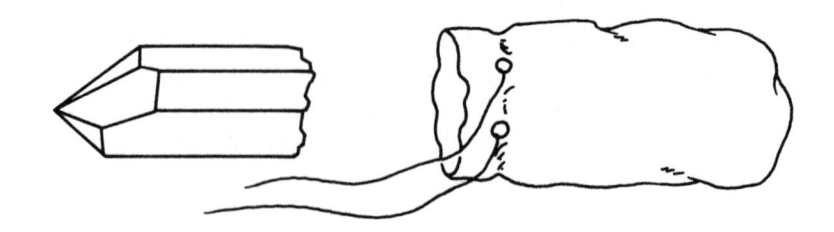

STANDS

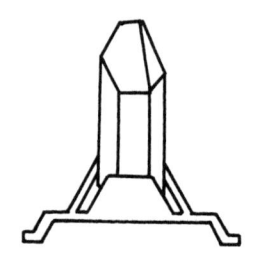

HEATSINKS

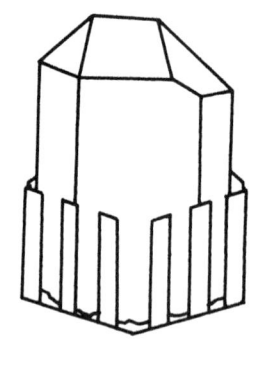

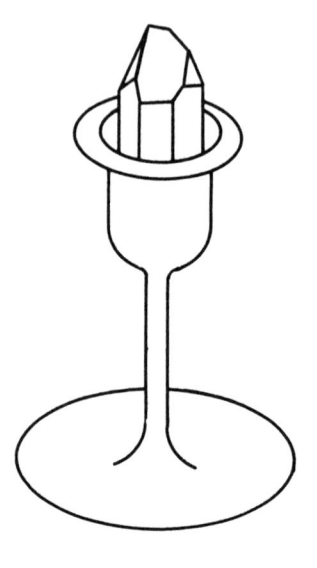

CRYSTAL AND LEATHER ACCESSORIES

For those of you who like to wear your crystals and are looking for new and different ways to keep these aura amplifiers with you at all times, we've come up with some interesting combinations of leather and crystals. Whether you wear these accessories for everyday, ceremonial purposes, on motorcycle outings, at a Star Trek convention or Halloween party, they're bound to improve your outlook while increasing your enjoyment of whatever you're doing.

Another added benefit of these crystal accessories is their aura enhancement effect. These crystal tools are also aura amplifiers, that raise your vibrational level. This is a real plus, especially if your aura is already influenced by positive thoughts and emotions. Like other crystal tools, these accessories are going to amplify your energy and intensify your experiences.

Your adventure into crystal and leather accessories is limited only by your imagination, which is always in the act of creation. We've given some basic designs that can provide a springboard for your own creative impulses to personalize and individualize your creations until they reflect your own unique personality.

As an added benefit, many of these projects can be made with leather from old purses, wallets, belts, vests, jackets, etc. This is a good way to recycle items that would otherwise go to waste and save money at the same time.

AURAL HEADBAND

The aural headband is one of the most versatile accessories using crystal and leather. Constructed as a headband, it can also be worn as a neckband, a hatband, and even as a garter under your clothing.

The only materials needed for this project are a quartz crystal and some medium soft leather. You will also need a pair of scissors, a leather punch and epoxy glue. This headband is much easier to construct and more versatile than the early copper and crystal headbands described in *Crystal Power*.

CRYSTAL WARRIOR

Materials:

A. Quartz crystal, 2" long by 3/4" diameter

B. Leather for headband, 2" wide by 20" long

C. Leather for crystal mounting frog, 9-1/2" by 5-1/4"

D. Leather thong or shoe lace, 24" long

E. Epoxy glue, suitable for gluing leather

Construction:

1. Cut the leather for the headband, 2" wide by 20" long (B).

2. Use epoxy glue to glue down 1/2" all along either side of the length of the headband as shown by the dotted lines in the diagram. Use clips or a heavy object to hold the headband flat while the glue dries.

3. Punch two holes at either end of the headband about 1/2" apart for the leather thong to lace through.

4. Punch five more holes in the center of the headband as shown in the diagram. The top two holes should be 3/4" apart and the center hole of the bottom three should be at the exact center of the headband.

5. Cut the crystal mounting frog (C) according to the diagram. The center section that holds the crystal should measure 1-1/4" by 1-1/2" and the five legs of the frog should each measure 4" and be cut 1/4" thick and trimmed to a point at the ends. The five legs of the mounting frog will lace through the five holes in the center of the headband.

6. Pick a quartz crystal about 2" long and approximately 3/4" in diameter to mount on the headband. The base of the crystal may need to be smoothed off so it doesn't have any rough edges that could cut or puncture the leather. This can be done by tapping the sharp edges gently with a hammer and using a file or rasp for smoothing.

7. Insert the five legs of the mounting frog into the five holes on the headband. Pull them all the way through and insert the crystal into the pocket formed by the frog. Tie the bot-

tom three legs together securely at the back of the headband. The top two legs can be wrapped around the crystal and inserted back through the top two holes in the band a second time before they are tied at the back for a tighter fit, if necessary. All the thongs are then tied together in back to finish off the mounting.

8. Insert the 24" leather thong through the two holes on one side of the headband, as shown in the diagram. To wear the headband, thread the thongs through the holes on the opposite side of the headband and tie them for a snug fit.

AURAL HEADBAND

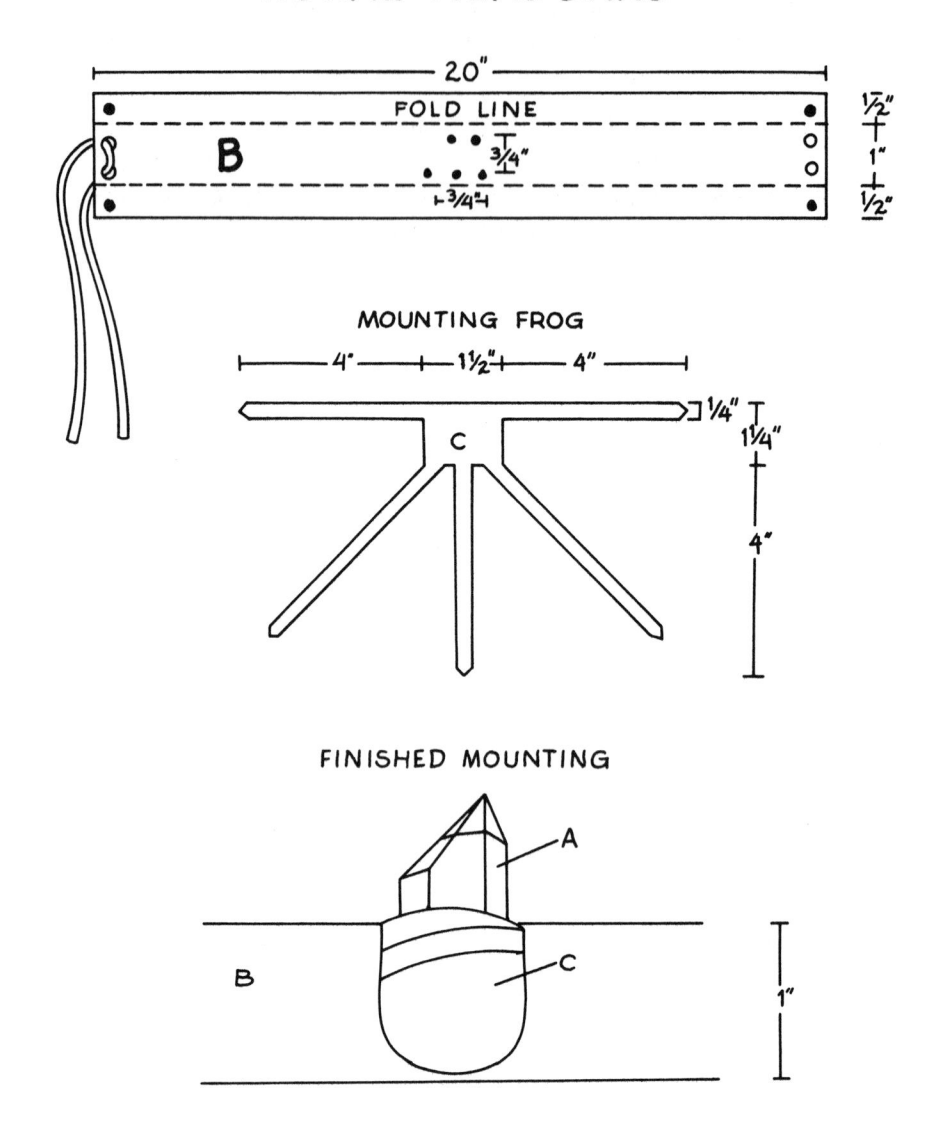

B — 20" × 2" (½" + 1" + ½"), with fold line; holes marked at 3/4" spacing

MOUNTING FROG — C: 4" + 1½" + 4", height 1¼" (¼" + 1"), legs 4"

FINISHED MOUNTING — A (crystal), B (band), C (frog), 1"

WARRIOR ARMBAND

The warrior armband is easy to construct and is a striking addition to any wardrobe or costume. The directions given here are for one armband, but some people prefer to make two of these, one for each arm. The armband was designed to fit on the lower arm, but with a few adjustments to the size of the leather you cut, it can easily be adapted to fit the upper arm. All the materials, except the crystal, can be acquired at leather supply stores.

NOTE: Before you cut the main piece of leather, draw the specifications out on a sheet of paper. Cut your pattern out and try it on your arm to fit 1" above your wrist or where you'll be wearing it on your upper arm. At this point, the pattern can easily be altered, if necessary.

Materials:

A. Leather, fairly heavy and sturdy, 6-1/2" along the top, 9" along the bottom, by 5" wide (see diagram)

B. Two leather straps, 2-1/2" long by 1" wide, rounded on ends

C. Leather crystal holder, 4-1/2" long by 1" wide, rounded on ends

D. Quartz crystal, 2-1/2" long with a 3/4" diameter

E. Two screw-in buffalo nickel conchas, or others of a similar size

F. Four sets of leather snaps

Construction:

1. Cut the four pieces of leather (A, B, C) to the sizes specified.

2. Punch two holes at one end of the wristband (A), about 1/2" in from the end and 3/4" in from the sides where one set of snaps will go.

3. Punch a hole in either end of each of the leather strips (B), about 1/2" in from the ends.

4. Attach one set of snaps to hold the straps on the wristband.

5. Attach the male half of the second set of snaps to the free end of the straps, 1/2" in from the ends.

6. Position the crystal (D) in the center of the wristband (A) and punch holes on either side of it, approximately 1-3/4" apart. Fit the leather crystal-holder strap (C) over the crystal and punch two more holes in the strap to match those on the wristband. Screw in the nickel conchas on either side of the crystal, through both the strap (C) and the wristband (A), so that they hold the crystal tightly in place.

7. You are now ready to insert the female half of the last set of snaps. Try the wristband on again to make sure of the placement, then punch holes and insert the snaps.

NOTE: This finishes the basic wristband. Other decorations and different types of conchas can be added to further personalize it if you wish.

Aura Amplifiers and Accessories 117

WARRIOR ARMBAND

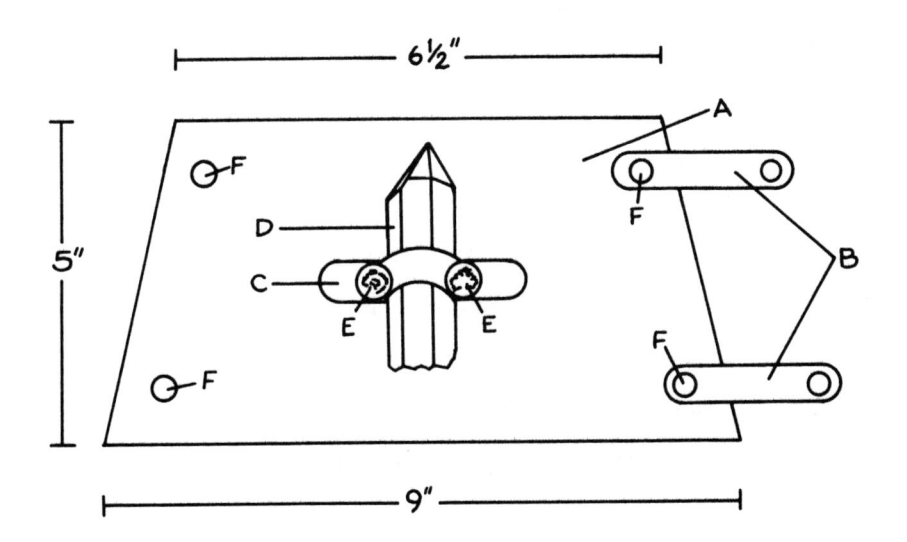

AMAZON ANKLET OR CHOKER

The leather and crystal anklet can make a snappy addition to any outfit for either sex. The anklet can be worn over or under jeans or pants, on the bare leg, or over boots. The anklet shown here is made of maroon leather and is designed to be worn on a bare leg. The anklet ties about 1-3/4" above the ankle and the main body of the anklet should measure about the same or just slightly less than the measurement around that spot on your ankle, pants or boot. Using a longer piece of leather and a slightly smaller crystal, this pattern can easily be altered to make a leather and crystal choker to be worn around the neck.

Materials:

  A. A strip of medium weight leather cut 17" long by 3" wide (adjust the length, according to where it will be worn)

  B. Leather strip, cut 4" long by 1" thick, rounded on ends

  C. Quartz crystal, approximately 2" long by 3/4" diameter

  D. Two buffalo nickel screw-in conchas

  E. Four small metal leather rivets

  F. Epoxy glue, suitable for gluing leather

Construction:

1. Cut the anklet leather (A) as shown in the diagram. The two tie pieces are cut 1/4" thick out of the main body of the leather. The center portion should measure 9" long (or the distance 1-3/4" above your ankle on your bare leg, pants, or boot) by 3" wide. Fold 3/4" down along the length of each side of the anklet to form a seam at the center of the back. Seen from the front, the pieces that tie will now be near the center of the anklet with the wrong side of the leather facing you.

2. Cut leather strip (B), rounding the ends.

3. Place the crystal (C) in the center of the anklet and punch holes on either side of it (approximately 1-1/2" apart). Posi-

tion leather strip (B) over the crystal and punch two more holes in it to match those below (approximately 2-1/2" apart).

4. Insert the crystal and screw in the conchas on either side of the leather to hold the crystal tightly in place.

5. Try on the anklet with the crystal in place and the ties fastened at the back of your leg. If the main body of the anklet is too long to tie nicely, cut the leather back slightly until you get a good fit.

6. Insert two rivets for reinforcement at each end of the anklet where the ties emerge from the folded leather.

AMAZON ANKLET

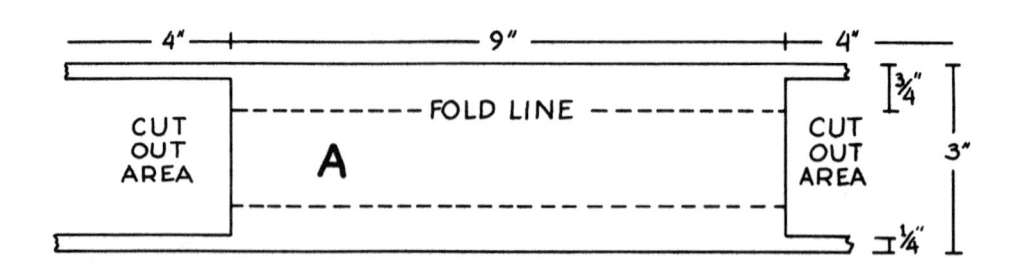

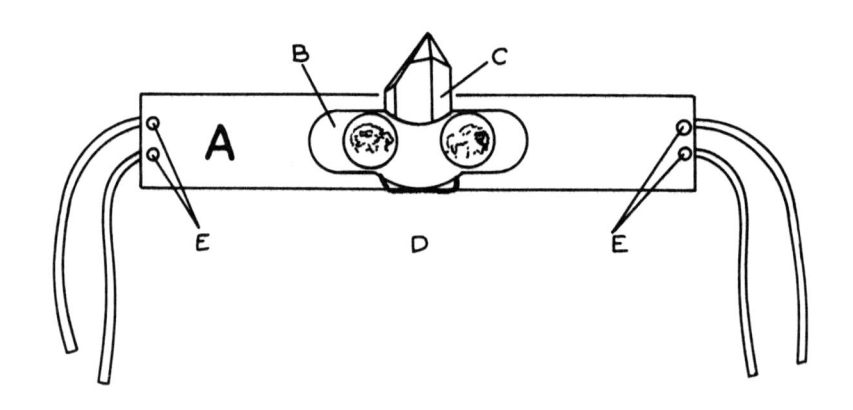

MYSTIC GAUNTLETS AND OTHER ACCESSORIES

Any pair of good quality leather gloves that extend back beyond the wrist can be magically transformed into aura-enhancing mystic gauntlets by the addition of a crystal. Use the tie-on mounting shown for the headband or the leather strip and screw-on mounting used for the wristband and anklet. In a similar manner, crystals can be attached to belts, vests, bags, purses, jackets, leather briefcases. Small crystals can also be easily applied using just epoxy to any of the above items, or any others your imagination comes up with.

CRYSTAL MASK

The crystal mask is one of the easier items to assemble and leaves lots of leeway for creativity. A simple Lone Ranger type mask can be acquired at a costume shop, or almost anywhere during the Halloween season. Wrap-around masks can also be made of leather or cloth in the style of Zorro or Batman.

Materials:

A. Black Lone Ranger type mask

B. Triangle of leather, painted, 2-1/2" base by 3" height (optional)

C. Silver or turquoise decorations (optional)

D. Quartz crystal, 1" to 1-1/4" long by 1/2" diameter

E. Copper tape, 1/4" wide for mounting crystal

F. Instant bonding glue

Construction:

Your particular mask can be as individual as you are. For ours, we cut out a triangle of leather and painted it with a circle design in red, white, and black. Modeling paints can be used or, if you don't have any handy, try using white correction fluid with a red and a black magic marker. The triangle was glued to the mask, using instant bonding glue, positioning the point over the nose piece. The crystal was then glued over the triangle, with the tip resting on the nosepiece, and copper tape was wrapped over the crystal and through the eye holes to hold it securely. To finish it off, a turquoise stone was glued in the center of the circle on the triangle and smaller turquoise and silver decorations were glued to the outer circle.

Aura Amplifiers and Accessories 123

CRYSTAL MASK

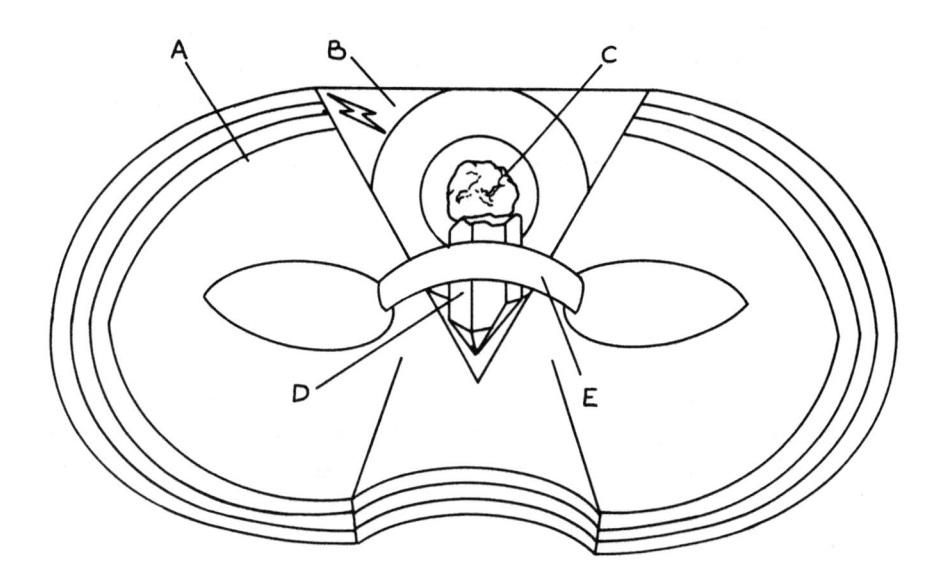

A
B
C
D
E

METAL AND CRYSTAL ACCESSORIES

For centuries, people have worn gold, silver, copper, brass and bronze accessories. These metals, and others, have also been used with gems to create beautiful jewelry. Below, we've given you two creative ways to combine metal with aura-amplifying crystals. The metals in these accessories are excellent conductors of crystal energy for a more powerful amplification of your aura. Using the two methods described here to attach the crystals, you could also add crystals to helmets, shields, or other metal accessories. If you wear a neck, back or leg brace, a small crystal glued on in a place where it won't interfere with the apparatus or get knocked off can help you boost your own healing energy.

POWER WRISTBANDS

The power wristband is a great way to enhance your aura. In addition, it's a striking accompaniment to any costume or outfit. For a super hero look, make two of these and wear one on each arm. Like the warrior armband, the power wristband can be adapted to be worn on the upper arm.

Materials:

A. Copper cup, or a sheet of copper 7-3/4" by 4"

B. 3/4" copper end cap

C. Quartz crystal, 2" long by 3/4" diameter

D. A small nut and bolt

E. Copper tape and instant bonding glue

Construction:

1. The wristband pictured here was fashioned from a copper cup. However, if you can't find one, you can buy a flat sheet of copper and, with a little extra bending and folding, produce the same wristband.

2. Remove the handle, which is usually soldered on, from the cup by bending it back and forth until it comes off.

3. Using tin snips, cut out about a 3/4" wide strip lengthwise. Start at the open end of the cup and cut on either side of the solder spots where the handle was mounted.
4. Cut the bottom off the cup.
5. If the cup has straight sides, you will want to angle the sides so that it will be narrower at the end nearest your wrist. Angle the cut so that the circumference of the cup at the wrist end is at least 1" smaller than the other end. This will make the wristband fit the shape of your arm better than straight sides would.
6. Smooth the raw edges of the bracelet with a file or a power grinder. Then fold 1/8" of all the raw edges over to the inside of the wristband, bending with a pair of needle-nose pliers. Hammer the edges flat using a small hammer and anvil.
7. Try on the wristband and bend it smaller, by squeezing, to fit your wrist and arm.
8. Once the wristband fits, the crystal mounting can be attached. Drill a hole towards the bottom of the side of the copper end cap (B) and a matching one on the wristband far enough down so the end cap with its crystal will be centered lengthwise on the wristband.
9. Bolt the end cap to the wristband with the head of the bolt inside the wristband and the nut inside the end cap.
10. Mount the crystal in the end cap using a copper tape shim. When you're satisfied with the fit, pour instant bonding glue in to form a secure mounting. The wristband is ready to wear as soon as the glue is dry.

Comments:

The wristband is finished at this point, but if you want something really unique, metal or stone pieces can be glued on the wristband in whatever design you choose. For example, a pair of lightening bolts in silver or brass on either side of the crystal are a really nice touch. When you're searching for decorations for the power wristband or other accessories, in addition to looking in craft or jewelry shops, take a look at your own jewelry. Part of an old piece that you no longer wear may be perfect to dress up an accessory. The unlikeliest sources often provide the best inspirations when people are working on crystal creations, so try to view pieces and parts of things that you have laying around in a new and different light.

POWER WRISTBAND

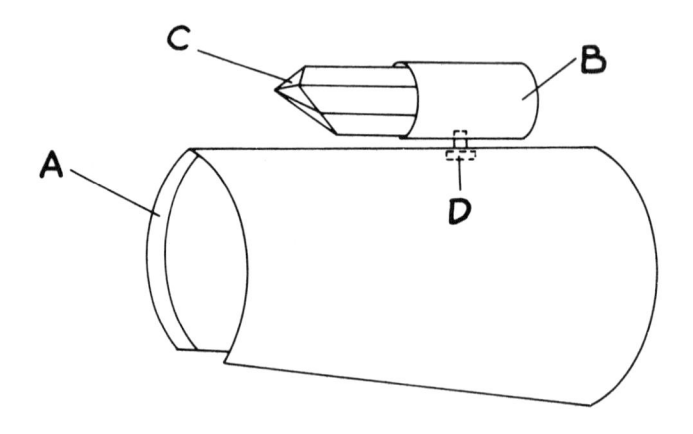

ENERGY BRACELETS

These energy bracelets are not only easy to make, but they're attractive enough to arouse the envy of Wonder Woman and other super heroes. To make these bracelets you need two plain metal bracelets 1" or so wide. The bracelets can be made from any metal you choose: copper, brass, silver, etc. You can find them at jewelry stores, garage sales, or perhaps among your own jewelry.

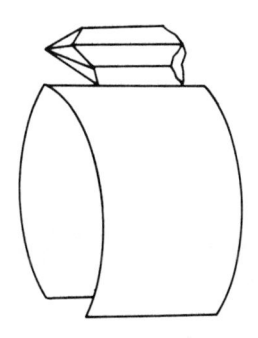

Next, you need two crystals. They should be no longer than the width of the bracelets and have one fairly flat side. Use jewelry epoxy to glue the flattest sides of the crystals directly on the bracelets. Don't skimp on the amount of glue you use because you want to get a good solid bond. When the glue is dry, presto, you have a pair of bracelets that can be worn with everyday clothes or for dress-up occasions.

ENERGY BRACELETS

PART III

EARTH ENERGIES

The key to all human endeavors is the Earth and her energies. Everything can be traced back to the Earth Mother/Father. Many of the energies we work with come from the Earth Source. The materials that make up our bodies are also of the Earth. If we want to grow and expand our consciousness, we must become aware of and in tune with the Earth, the breath of the living being that supports us.

In the following section, we'll explore how the crystal garden and crystal arranging will expand our awareness of how the Earth and her rhythms work. We will see how making and/or wearing crystal jewelry helps us take our new awareness with us wherever we are. We'll investigate both the dangers and advantages of making and using the aggressive shield, and see how the household shield can improve our lives. In the pursuit of physical and mental health, the chapter on the crystal water of life explains exactly how you can inexpensively produce, right in your own home, crystal water charged with negative ions. And finally, we will penetrate the Power and the Spirit with complete directions for performing the Native American pipe ceremony and healing circle to enrich the Earth and all our lives.

Chapter 12

CRYSTAL GARDEN AND CRYSTAL ARRANGING

Crystals, like other living beings, need love.

CRYSTAL ROCK GARDEN

A crystal rock garden is a beautiful addition to any home. It can be as large or small as you want it to be. We used an area of seventeen feet by twenty-two feet, about half of our patio/courtyard area, for ours. The rock garden allows us to pursue two of our favorite hobbies at the same time, rock hunting and gardening.

The garden started, almost accidentally, on the unbricked portion of our courtyard when we realized that our house lacked sufficient space to display all the rocks that we'd gathered over the years. Those special rocks and crystals were used to circle the top of a mound of dirt and a plant was put in the center of the circle. We then used the area as a focus for pipe ceremonies.

The effect was so nice, that we began to gather more rocks every time we went to the mountains or country. We used the rocks to surround planting beds for vegetables and flowers that seemed appropriate to the area, which was partially shaded by tall hedges on two sides. Old pieces of flagstone were formed together in a wandering mosaic to provide pathways through the garden.

It turned out that the strawberries loved their space so much that by fertilizing and pulling out half the plants each time they produced, we could get two abundant crops of strawberries each season without ever having to replace the plants every two or three years as is recommended. Another rounded space houses a variety of vegetables each year, leftovers from the main garden.

Then there are the flowers. Marigolds scattered among the rocks and a formal flower bed of perennials add bright spots of color and green in odd spaces.

But the best part of the garden is the part we didn't plan. After the first year of tedious weed-pulling to get rid of literally thousands of sapling elm, and other unidentified trees that decided to grow among our rocks, smaller volunteer plants began to appear between the rocks from the rich mulch left over when the trees lost their leaves and crumbled too fine to be blown away. Small ground covers began growing between the flagstones and rocks, happy to provide a softening touch of green. English ivy, woodbine and periwinkle covered the area under the bushes in a soft mat of green with purple flowers. The woodbine was trained over tomato cages and an arched gate for more privacy.

Then there were the surprise plants that came to live in our rock garden: there was a luminaria, or silver dollar plant, that insisted on growing among the rocks by the front porch, creating purple flowers in the spring and golden silver dollars in the fall; the white acorn squash that miraculously appeared on a flagstone path to wander among the strawberries; the pak choi (a Chinese plant similar to cabbage) that sprung up next to the sidewalk; the giant sunflower that grew from the seeds we feed the squirrels; occasional watermelons and tender lettuces that emerged here and there. Every year new volunteer plants are attracted to this space and have to be allowed to grow and express their own particular beauty. Now, very few weeds have to be pulled and the rock garden is a constantly changing montage of color and life.

The rock garden even seems to attract only beneficial insects and bugs. Other than slugs in the strawberries the first year, there hasn't been any insect damage. Of course we use only compost and manure with no sprays or chemicals to pollute our garden and it's as if the Earth is establishing her own wonderful balance in a spot that allows every mineral, plant and life form to express to its fullest with a vigor that is an astonishing and abundant expression of her own harmony.

The idea behind our rock garden was to create an area of beauty and peace so that we could enjoy nature right at home in the city. We borrowed the design from the Eastern concepts of yin and yang in relation to the Earth energy of our home and yard. Most homes and yards are laid out in straight lines, squares and rectangles. Too many of these shapes can cause an unnatural and unbalanced flow of energy in the Earth's magnetic field. One way to balance the energy for a healthy home environment is by building a rock garden using curving patterns and mounds. This can balance the yin/yang energy.

Circles of rocks can be used to surround the areas where plants and flowers grow. Flagstone walkways can be laid out in gently curving lines. Rounded rock or brick borders can also be used around flower beds that grow along the straight side of the house.

All kinds of natural rocks lend themselves to use along the borders of the planting beds and walkways. The natural variations in the shapes of the rocks helps to balance the energy of the Earth garden. Even the flagstones used for the walkways can be can be different shapes and sizes. Some will have straight line edges, but not all. The various shapes can be fitted together to form curving walkways.

Some areas for plants can be irregular forms like kidney shapes, oblongs or half moons. The areas don't need to be exact circles or ovals. Mounds and small hills can be used to vary the elevation of the ground in different areas of the garden. These mounds should have gently sloping sides, not steep or sharp angles. Like the enclosures, these mounds need not be an exact circle and they can be enhanced by a variety of rocks in the surrounding borders.

The best way to gather rocks for your garden is to hunt them yourself in the countryside over a period of time. This enables you to use a variety of colors, shapes and sizes to add interest and texture to your garden. If that isn't possible and you need to buy your rocks from landscape or gravel companies, get as much variety as you can in the rocks you purchase. Try to make each rock, large or small, a special expression of your unique individuality.

Crystals can be added to your garden in a variety of ways to increase the harmonic vibrations. One way is to glue a crystal to the top of a smooth river rock or piece of white quartz. Or you can build small crystal rods to stick in the ground. Crystals can also be buried any place in the garden where you want there to be a particular focal point of energy; or if you're reluctant to trust your crystals to the elements, just take a bowl of crystals or a rod out with you to place in the garden while you're enjoying it or using it for meditation and bring them in later. The crystals and the rocks in the garden will interact and charge each other and balance out their energies and your own in a special way.

We work with the Earth and the Earth works with us when we create a rock garden as a center of light and energy. People, plants, birds, animals, insects and the Earth all meet and enjoy the sanctuary of a rock garden as a harmonious whole that expresses unconditional love.

CRYSTAL AND ROCK ARRANGING

A crystal arrangement can be a rock garden on a smaller scale inside your home. Crystal arrangements are easy to do, even easier than flower arranging. A base plate, shallow basket or bowl is chosen first. Plates of silver, copper or brass are easily found at garage sales if you want to do it economically. We usually do. Shallow baskets also work well for display. The plate or basket can be lined on the bottom with a circle of dark colored velvet to provide a contrast for the crystals. Black, maroon, dark blue, or forest green (depending on the color scheme of your room) all work well. Once you've chosen your container and lined it, what do you put in it? Most of us have more than a few "favorite" rocks and crystals sitting around the house. In fact, many of us have attracted so many favorites that choosing which to use for our arrangement may be difficult. Not to worry. Just make more arrangements with them. The ways they can be used for decoration are infinite. A big advantage of arranging the rocks and crystals in groups is that they take up less space than when they sit around separately. Also, our mineral kingdom friends enjoy each other's company in groups and putting them together creates a new and unique energy vortex for the home. The arrangement can even provide a miniature temple, altar or circle for prayer and meditation. Beauty and peace radiate from these artistic arrangements. The rocks and crystals can be chosen by physical sight and intuition simultaneously. If you listen carefully, they will tell you which of them will blend harmoniously in an arrangement.

Describing any particular arrangement is difficult, because each one is as individual and unique as the rocks, crystals and the person arranging them, but we'll to give you a few examples of things we've tried.

If you're intent on raising your vibrations quickly, you'll want a bedside table arrangement. However, if you're very sensitive to the vibrations of crystals or are new to them, they may make it difficult to sleep at first and you may need to move them closer gradually. We have several of these arrangements and use our most powerful crystals and rocks for them so that we can raise our vibrations while we sleep. One favorite is in a small antique silver candy dish with a circle of velvet to protect the bottom of the dish from scratching. There are eleven clear crystals of varying shapes and sizes: single and double terminated, twins, crystals with windows, doorways, ghosts and inclusions. Set amongst them are one each of orange citrine, amethyst, a blue crystal twin that has been irradiated with gold, several smoky quartz crystals (one included with amazonite), a large twin herkimer diamond, a yellow apatite and a watermelon tourmaline. There is also one each of polished carnelian, jasper, ruby, lapis and rose quartz, and a natural iron pyrite cluster. The larger crystals point outwards in a circle, with smaller crystals in the center standing upright. The polished rocks nestle atop and among the crystals providing contrast, additional color and a wonderful balance of energy. The iron pyrite cluster in the center boosts the energy of the whole arrangement. This arrangement is a particularly powerful one and takes up a minimum of space for the variety of energies you get. You may want to start out with something much simpler, giving you and the crystals time to attune to each other and gradually build up to something more complex.

Another favorite arrangement that graces our glass coffee table in the living room uses a flat copper dish with an abalone shell of pink, purple, turquoise and black braced upright on one side of the dish. An assortment of crystals and rock specimens spill out of the shell onto the dish, looking as if nature had arranged them, but actually carefully placed to display each to best advantage.

Abalone shells make wonderful containers for crystals in a variety of ways. If your table space is limited, a wire strings conveniently through one of the holes that walk up one side of the shell. The shell can be hung on the wall and the bottom pocket will hold a cluster and large amethyst that peek intriguingly out of their shell cave. The shells can also be laid flat and arranged with a display.

For larger rock specimens and crystals that you want to display to advantage there are endless variations. We use several rules for these arrangements that seem to work and you may think up others of your own that suit your taste. The first is not to crowd them so each can be admired as an individual. In a few cases just one piece may be displayed alone, such as a large amethyst cluster, but for the most part we use them in natural-looking groupings with wooden statues, plants, distressed wood, shells and other objects that allow the viewer to see a story in the arrangement. When doing these story groupings it's best to use uneven numbers of objects and asymmetry because this provides interest and stimulates the imagination. For example an antique Chinese inkstand in the shape of a dragon holds a large amethyst in the glass inkwell and an orange citrine nestles in the curve of the dragon's body. In another, a ceramic toad peeks over a geode in a spider plant, while a wooden carved antelope and hippopotamus look out from behind the plant's drooping fronds. On a windowsill, a Japanese statue watches from behind an oblong black rock that encloses a crystal-cluster cave, and another shorter rounded rock, flattened on the front, shows the shape of a robed lady resting against the taller rock.

If you have a bonsai plant, you have the perfect medium to tell a story. Unfortunately, a bonsai can take years to grow yourself and is expensive to buy. However, if you want instant gratification, you can have a beautiful bonsai in a very short time without a big money investment. Buy a juniper bush, the kind that people grow in front of their houses and sometimes trim like poodles, at any local garden center. Get the one with the most twisty, tortured looking trunk you can find. This is the way they grow naturally, so it shouldn't be difficult to find one. Preferably you can find one that will exactly suit the size of the container that you choose to put it in. Our container is a red clay bowl-shaped planter with a dish underneath.

The bush can be trimmed to its basic bonsai shape at any time of the year, so you can start trimming away the branches from the base of the plant as soon as you get it. Take it slowly and try to emulate the tortured shapes of trees growing out of bare rock on a mountain or one that has been wind-twisted on the plains. For re-potting you should wait until early spring before new growth starts.

Re-potting can be tricky, so if you're a beginner, to be on the safe side, choose a container where you won't have to trim away too much of the tap root or root hairs. Most junipers come in tall thin planting pots, so if you want a shorter wider permanent container, lay it at an angle to accommodate more of the roots and you can also leave a portion of the roots exposed.

Once the bush is trimmed you have an instant bonsai and when it's re-potted you can begin to tell a story with it. Different colored rock specimens broken into small pieces with a hammer make a nice variation on moss for a ground cover. (Be sure to wear glasses of some sort when smashing the rocks to protect your eyes and use a wooden frame to keep the chips from scattering,) Our bonsai has a large rock with small crystals growing out of it placed at the base of the tree; a realistic ceramic toad approaches the welcome shade and protection of the tree and the rock from the other side of the planter.

Whatever story you choose to tell with your arrangements, use a variety of textures, heights and shapes together so that the viewer will stop and become a part of your story for a moment. The principles are the same used in creating any kind of art or literature. You want to draw the observer out of his everyday life and create a fantasy that makes him expand his view of the world. Every one of us has the ability to create art in our own homes that will supersede the mundane details of everyday life and lead us into the realms of the spiritual.

The examples of rock arrangements we have given you will have, hopefully, fired up your imagination for creating something even more wonderful than what you've read about that uses your own favorite things and ideas. The materials are all around you and just waiting for you to put them to use. Try creating one today and experience the rich spiritual satisfaction of the artist.

Chapter 13

CRYSTAL JEWELRY

The jewel of the mind outshines that of the body.

From the beginning of time practitioners of the Earth religions have been using jewelry to assist in their ceremonies and to boost their personal energy. The kinds of jewelry used are as many and varied as the individual practitioners.

If you have a piece of jewelry that you want to wear for spiritual purposes or use in a ceremony, it can easily be cleansed and charged by putting it in the middle of the circle during a healing or prayer ceremony (outlined in Chapter 15). Any kind of jewelry that you like to wear is good for charging with energy. This applies whether you buy it, make it, or receive it as a gift.

Turquoise and silver jewelry, of the Native American kind, is one of the favorites among shamans and other Earth-oriented practitioners. New styles using silver with quartz crystals, rose quartz, lapis lazuli, amethyst and a host of other stones are also quite popular. Custom-made and designed jewelry in both silver and gold is also good for the craft if the practitioner has a higher budget. Necklaces, bracelets, pendants and earrings are all used for decoration and spiritual uses. Watchbands, headbands and anklets are now becoming popular as well.

All types of jewelry can be charged mentally or with prayer to radiate a peaceful protective aura around a person's body. And all jewelry can be programmed or asked to send healing energy to another person, plant or animal at any distance. The distance can be a few feet or hundreds of miles; the energy projected will still get there instantly.

Different kinds of stones of many colors can be worn in jewelry for other effects besides decoration. Red colors radiate quick earthy energy, pink the spread of love, green and blue are healing or calming, and purple, clear or white colors help to achieve a higher spirituality.

Everyone has favorite stones and favorite colors of stones that make them feel good. There are numerous guides for crystals and gemstones available on the market, but keep in mind that this is a highly subjective area. Individuals are unique in many respects so that the general guidelines may be helpful in choosing combinations of stones to wear, but they aren't strict rules. The best indicator of what is right is what feels good to you. Likewise, jewelry and styles of mountings for your favorite stones are very personal choices.

Primitive medicine bags are a favorite along with basic silver rings and pendants on silver chains. Some people prefer cut and faceted stones in custom-designed gold or silver pieces of jewelry. Whatever the style, the magic attraction of crystals and gemstones remains a universal constant from childhood, when we gathered our first lucky rocks. The wonder of our connections to the Earth through crystals, rocks and gemstones is a primitive natural energy that remains with us throughout our lives.

This ever-present connection to the Earth through jewelry reminds us that we can always send healing energy to the Earth through our stones and jewelry. A beam of energy can be sent to a plant, animal or person with just a thought through a crystal pendant or an amethyst ring. An energy field can be generated as an aura of protection with a thought and feeling of oneness through a turquoise and silver belt buckle. A charge of white light can be radiated from a pair of crystal earrings with a quick thought as you enter a room full of people.

In our search for spiritual growth, jewelry has always been

there to aid us on our path. As such, jewelry is another tool in this world of teachers and lessons that leads us to the light of self-knowledge. There are very few who would want to resist its beautiful and energy-enhancing help as we travel on life's journey.

JEWELRY MAKING

Many people prefer to make their own jewelry such as amulets, pendants, earrings, bracelets, necklaces, anklets and rings. Unless you have silver or gold-smithing skills, you'll probably choose to mount your stones in the variety of chains, fittings, and mountings available on the market. Abundant varieties of fittings are available at hobby, craft, or rock shops. Resin glues designed especially for jewelry are readily available at the above shops or hardware stores. Necklaces or earrings can easily be made using nothing more specialized than glue, fittings, and a pair of needle-nosed pliers. We encourage you to make some of your own jewelry with your favorite stones and crystals, as we have, so that you can experience the thrill of creating something uniquely yours that is programmed with your own special energy.

Chapter 14

AGGRESSIVE AND HOUSEHOLD SHIELDS

Love is a circle, with no beginning and no end.

AGGRESSIVE SHIELD

The aggressive shield is something that has been requested by many readers. It combines a single crystal programmed to radiate an energy field that acts as a shield, using the electronic circuitry of a black box. Either a single or double terminated quartz crystal can be used in this device.

The shield is used to prevent us from absorbing the negative vibrations often present in mass consciousness (the sum of humanity's thoughts). Have you ever gone to sleep feeling pretty good, only to awake the next morning in a terrible mood? Or have you ever started off to work cheerful and happy? A few hours later, without having any major problems to deal with, you felt awful. These cases are due to the effect of mass consciousness on our own perceptions of the world. Our goal is to change the vibration of mass consciousness to a higher level and we're beginning to progress. But until the mass consciousness has risen a bit further, we need to be aware of how it can color our perceptions of the world.

However, be careful how you use this tool. The aggressive shield not only shields us from other's thoughts or mass consciousness, it also amplifies the thoughts of the sender and reflects them back. The shield is neutral. It can be programmed positively or negatively. Make sure your programming is a product of love and acceptance before using this device.

Materials:

  A. Plastic box, approximately 2" by 3" by 1"

  B. Toggle switch

  C. Jack and plug

  D. Quartz crystal to fit box

  E. Solid copper wire for coil, 12"

  F. Two capacitors and copper lead wires to connect coil, jack, switch and capacitors

  G. Electrical tape or solder as indicated in directions

Construction:

Any type of small plastic box can be used for this device, but the box must separate into two halves. Two holes are drilled in one end of the box. The holes should be the appropriate diameter for mounting the jack and switch.

The quartz crystal should be chosen after you acquire the plastic box so that you can be sure it will easily fit inside. At least 12" of copper wire are wound in a coil around the crystal. A lead wire with an inline capacitor is then attached to each end of the copper coil. The copper coil is attached to the crystal by wrapping a short length of electrical tape around the coil and crystal. The lead wires and capacitors are connected by twisting the wires together and wrapping the connections with small strips of electrical tape. The connections can also be soldered if you have a soldering iron.

One contact on the jack and the switch are connected with wire. A lead wire from one capacitor is connected to the other contact on the switch. The lead wire from the other capacitor is connected to the other contact on the jack.

Aggressive and Household Shields 145

AGGRESSIVE SHIELD

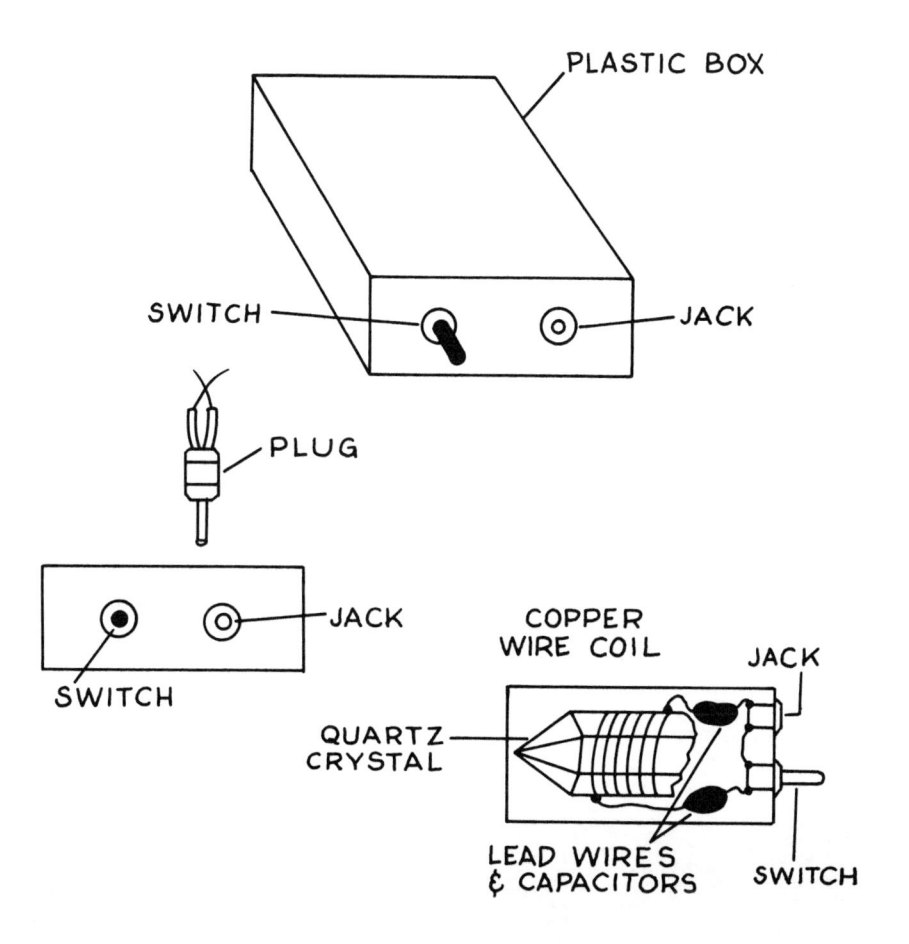

Once the wiring is complete, the two halves of the plastic box can be rejoined by glue or screws.

The last item is the plug with leads to plug into the jack. The lead wires should be connected and twisted together. These wires can be soldered or twisted and taped with electrical tape to form a connection. This plug and jack make a quick disconnect circuit. The switch must be on and the jack plugged in to activate the unit.

HOUSEHOLD SHIELD

The aggressive shield, while drawing much interest, may be a bit much for some people. There's another way to provide a more passive energy-balancing shield for your home, garden and property with the household shield. The basic element of the household shield is a crystal egg. The egg is a traditional symbol of Earth energy, both masculine and feminine, stemming from the fact that all of us begin our physical lives as eggs. This ageless symbol of birth and life literally comes alive when charged and programmed by a human being with the life force energy.

A crystal egg can be used by itself on a plastic, wooden or metal holder as a household shield. Even though it's shaped and polished, the crystal egg has the same "live" atomic structure as any other quartz crystal. This is the part that will respond to your thoughts, emotions, and spiritual self. It reflects and amplifies the sum total of your consciousness and conscious awareness while helping you expand that consciousness and awareness.

Once you've chosen your crystal egg, hold it in the hand that feels best to you while you program it. The programming is done the same way you would program any other crystal tool. The method we use is to close our eyes and sense the energy aura in the egg expanding until it encompasses the house and yard in a white-light bubble of peace and harmony.

This type of programming insures that our property will feel uncomfortable to anyone who has negative vibrations or larcenous intentions. Rather than invade a space that feels so uncomfortable, that type of person will instinctively go elsewhere. It's almost as if our property is invisible to them. It also makes our property appeal to the higher-level portions of the mind of anyone who is nearby and can help them expand their consciousness to a higher level if they choose to.

Living in an inner city neighborhood, as we do, robberies and street gang violence are common events for some of our out-of-balance neighbors, but not us. With our crystals, our gardens, and our attitude, we've created an island of peace and love where we live. Sometimes it's hard to believe stories of the violence that surrounds us because our home and visitors are so serene. We attribute this calm, not only to the household shields we use, but to our hard work in programming our own minds to love and harmony. In order to program our eggs with a peaceful aura we must first feel that way ourselves. This doesn't mean that we're always paragons of peace and love. Like everyone, we have some days that are better than others, but we strive to keep our thoughts loving as often as possible. It must work because, as a result, anyone entering our space responds to the love that encompasses our home, or stays away if that's not where they're at. It's always a surprise and joy when someone who looks like they could kill with never a thought, pauses to admire our garden and chat about plants or spiritual matters. It's also taught us not to be so quick to judge others by their appearance.

The crystal egg can also be used in conjunction with other crystals to create a household shield. Four single or double terminated crystals can be placed around the egg on its holder, with their tips pointing outward in the four directions. The egg and crystal arrangement can then be placed near the center of the house to act as a coordinator of the protective field formed by all the crystals.

The crystal egg for the household shield can be clear quartz or any of a variety of other quartz, such as milky, smoky, rose, amethyst or citrine. As always, pick a crystal egg that feels good to you.

Other variations on the basic household shield can include a crystal egg surrounded by different colored polished stones so that each stone can augment the egg's energy with the slightly different vibrations of each color of stone.

If you have quite a few polished eggs, you can create a household shield for every room of your home. One egg is powerful enough to protect your whole house and property, but with crystals and other beautiful works of nature, it's hard to stop at just one.

When you're deciding what kind of household shield to create, relax and give your creative mind and intuition free rein to tell you exactly what egg or combination of egg and rocks is right for your home. After that, make sure your mind is radiating peace and love when you program it and enjoy the results.

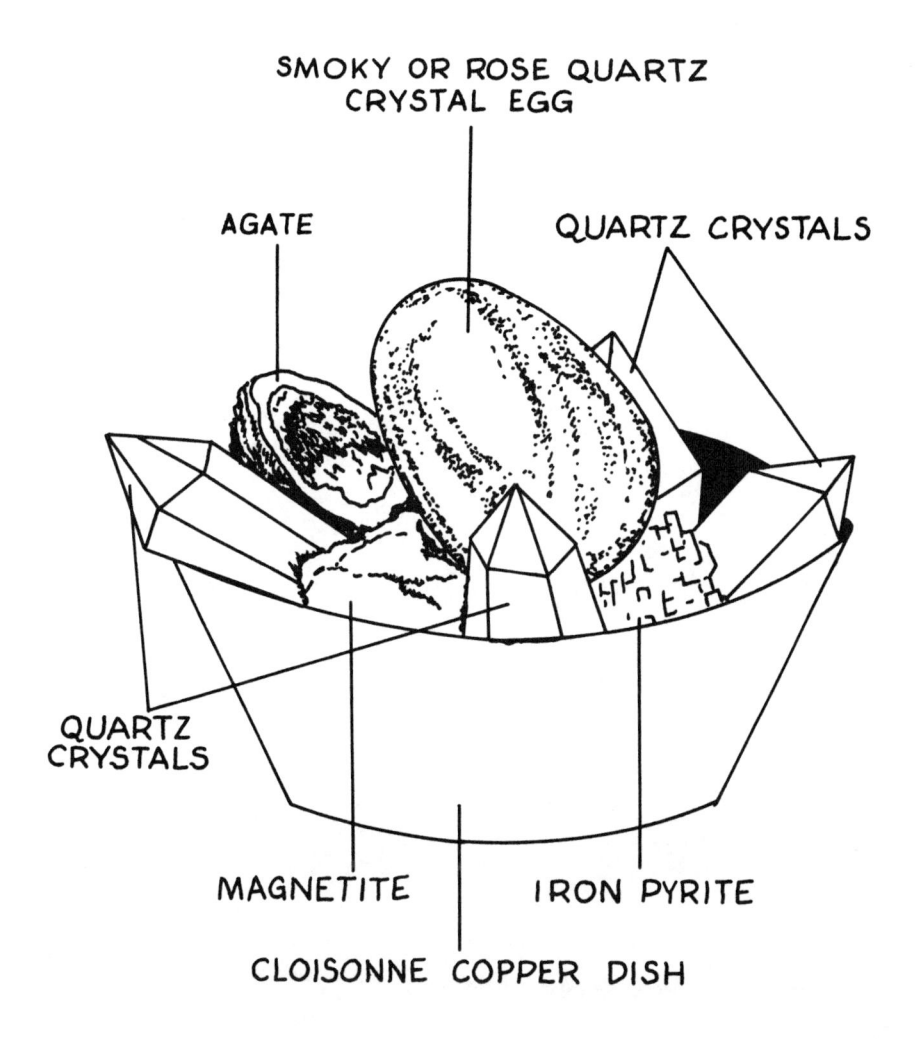

Aggressive and Household Shields 149

HOUSEHOLD SHIELD

- SMOKY OR ROSE QUARTZ CRYSTAL EGG
- AGATE
- QUARTZ CRYSTALS
- QUARTZ CRYSTALS
- MAGNETITE
- IRON PYRITE
- CLOISONNE COPPER DISH

Chapter 15

CRYSTAL WATER OF LIFE

*Knowledge is power, power is energy,
energy is balance and balance is healing.*

Many of us understand the balance of polarity in electricity, magnetics and ions. Positive and negative, in these cases are neither good nor bad, but simply descriptions of opposite forces. However, in general usage, negative means bad. This can become confusing when the subject is ions in the air because a concentration of positive ions is not healthy. The effects of this concentration are enervating and de-energizing. On the other hand, when there's a concentration of negative ions, such as in the presence of running water or right after a rainstorm, we feel more energetic, alive and positive.

Nion (pronounced ny-on) is the term we use for negative ion to avoid negative connotations. (The word is similar to the scientific term, anion, for the same thing, but has a more descriptive sound.) Machines that generate negative ions have become a popular item on the market in recent years. The next project uses two of these machines, a pyramid and crystals to energize drinking water right in your own home.

NION GENERATOR

This device is a bit more expensive to construct than many other crystal projects because it uses two negative ion generators. But it can pay for itself in a short time, making it well worth building. Once built, this machine can provide a steady source of energized crystal water for you, your family and friends for years to come. Since commercially available crystal water is very expensive, it provides you with a considerable savings to build your own generator of crystal-charged water.

Another advantage to building this machine is that, while the plans may look complex, it's actually very easy to put one together yourself because there are very few parts, and the ion generators and pyramids have been pre-assembled by someone else.

For this project, any size or model of commercially built negative ion generators will work. There are quite a variety of them on the market to choose from (perhaps you'll even be lucky enough to find them cheaply at garage sales). The pyramid used with this device can also vary in size or type, depending on the set-up you decide to use. The size of the nion generators and pyramid used also determines the size of the glasses used to hold the crystals and water. In order to prevent impurities in your tap water from interfering with the results, distilled water should be used.

Materials:

A. Two negative ion generators, any size

B. Two copper strips of a length sufficient to fit over generators to attach them to the base (optional)

C. Four screws to attach copper strips to base (optional)

D. Three glasses for water, 2-1/2" diameter by 4-1/2" height

E. Any pyramid with a 6" to 28" base

F. Wood base, 17" x 11" x 1", or size to fit generators (optional)

G. Distilled water

H. Ten to thirty small quartz crystals or a few larger ones

I. Covers of any kind to place over the glasses (optional)

Construction:

One of the nicest characteristics of this unit is not just the benefits of the crystal-energized water, but that it is so easily put together once you've purchased the negative ion generators. The simplicity of the assembly means, that with very little effort or time spent, you can have a complete working unit.

The two negative ion generators used measure 6-1/4" length by 2-1/4" height by 8" width. The generators shown in the diagram are strapped to a 17" by 11" wood base with 1" wide copper straps that are 16" long for ease of moving the unit. The straps are then attached to the base with 4 screws. If you plan to leave your unit in one place most of the time, the base is not necessary.

The space for the glass of crystals (or glasses of crystals, if you want to charge more than one at a time) between the machines measures 3-1/4". The water glasses shown are 2-1/2" in diameter and 4-1/2" high. One to three glasses can be used at a time, depending on how much water you want to treat. Different sizes of glasses can be used in glass or plastic. One effect we did notice with the nion generator was that the negative ions tended to attach themselves to dirt particles in the air and deposit them behind the machines. In order to protect the water being charged, you may want to put a covering over the glasses.

The pyramid can be large enough to fit over the entire unit (24" to 28" base) or just large enough to rest on the generators and cover only the glasses (6" to 8" base).

We use approximately 30 crystals (1" long by 1/4" in diameter) per glass. You can use more or less crystals with adequate results. You may also vary the size of the crystals. Smaller or larger crystals can certainly be used effectively. The crystals we use come from Arkansas or Brazil, but any clear quartz crystal will work. The crystals should be washed thoroughly before they are used in the water glasses.

The glasses, with the crystals, should be filled at least three-quarters full of water and covered, if you choose. Then, they are set between the nion generators and the pyramid is put in position over them.

When the unit is turned on, the water-charging cycle takes twenty-four hours. The process doesn't seem to improve by using a longer charging period, although it certainly won't hurt the water to charge it longer. If the water is going to be used right away, a twelve-hour charging period is adequate. When the charging is done, pour the water out of the charging glasses, making sure that the crystals don't slip out. (Swallowing a crystal would definitely not be beneficial to your health.) Now your nion-charged crystal water is ready to be used or stored.

THE BENEFITS OF NEGATIVE IONS

The natural balance of ions is four negative ions to five positive ions. Unfortunately, the balance of ions in the artificial environments of our buildings and our cars tends toward the positive. The natural balance, or even an overdose of negative ions, has been found to be beneficial and promotes health, both physically and emotionally. When there is an abundance of negative ions present people have been found to be more cheerful and energetic. Perhaps you've experienced this yourself near a waterfall, in the shower, or just after a rainstorm. They also have been found in tests to speed up the healing process for many ailments.

An added benefit of this device is that the generators clean and charge the air in the home environment as they work with the pyramid and crystals to charge the water.

NOTE: Occasionally too many negative ions can cause people to stay too alert and lose sleep, but it's easy to decrease the amount of nions in the air by turning the machines off at night or by keeping them away from sleeping areas.

SUGGESTED USES FOR CRYSTAL WATER OF LIFE

1. Drink a small amount of the water full strength each day, or dilute it in your regular drinking water, and observe the results in your health and attitude.

2. Wash your face or bathe sore muscle areas with the water. (For open sores and rashes don't neglect your usual medications.)

3. Water your plants with the water full strength or diluted and see how they perk up.

Crystal Water of Life 155

CRYSTAL WATER GENERATOR

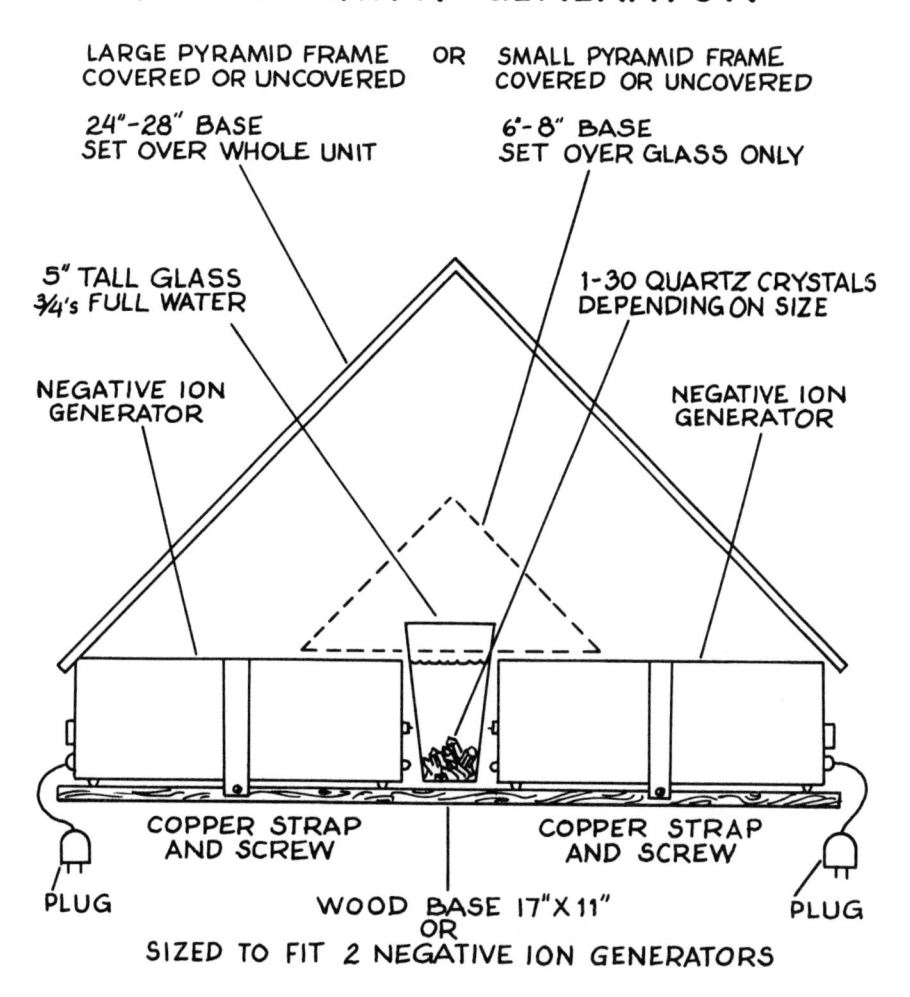

LARGE PYRAMID FRAME OR SMALL PYRAMID FRAME
COVERED OR UNCOVERED COVERED OR UNCOVERED

24"-28" BASE 6'-8" BASE
SET OVER WHOLE UNIT SET OVER GLASS ONLY

5" TALL GLASS 1-30 QUARTZ CRYSTALS
¾'s FULL WATER DEPENDING ON SIZE

NEGATIVE ION NEGATIVE ION
GENERATOR GENERATOR

COPPER STRAP COPPER STRAP
AND SCREW AND SCREW

PLUG PLUG
WOOD BASE 17"X 11"
OR
SIZED TO FIT 2 NEGATIVE ION GENERATORS

4. Pour a small amount in your bath water.

Comments:

The above suggestions are just a few ways you can experiment with your crystal water of life. The benefits of crystal nion-charged water haven't been fully explored yet, but from tests done, it's an exciting and promising area of research. The combination of crystals, a pyramid, water, and nions has many possibilities. The nion generator will allow you to explore the benefits of crystal-charged water, affordably, so that you can come to your own conclusions.

SIMPLE CRYSTAL-CHARGED WATER

For those of you who aren't inclined to go to the trouble or expense of building a nion generator, there's an easier way to experiment with the effects of crystals on drinking water. To do this, all you need do is pick a single crystal, wash it thoroughly and then place it in the bottom of the glass you drink water out of. Pour distilled water in the glass and let the crystal charge the water you drink throughout the day.

The size or shape of the crystal used isn't important, but there are a couple of considerations to take into account when choosing your water crystal. First, the crystal should be heavy enough that it will stay in the bottom of the glass, so you don't swallow it by mistake. The crystal we use is 1-1/2" long and 1/2" in diameter. Then, the straighter the sides and the smoother the bottom, the easier it is to wash clean before you use it and periodically during its use. After that, it's merely a matter of pouring the water in and drinking it.

The benefits of drinking water that is charged this way are hard to judge. As part of a healthy balanced dieting regimen, the authors were instructed to drink six to eight glasses of water a day. Not knowing how beneficial large amounts of tap water are to the system, distilled water was chosen. One day, while performing this daily duty, it occurred to them that one could get some of the benefits of the good energy of crystals by placing one in the bottom of the water glass.

Without making any outrageous claims as to the benefits, their health was great throughout the experiment and extra weight melted away gradually with very little effort. Whether the effects were the result of healthy eating habits, a good attitude, or the crystal, who knows. But, if nothing else, the sight of that crystal in the bottom of the glass just made them feel better and more positive about life and health. They also agreed that the crystal water tasted lots better than plain old distilled water.

We urge you to try this experiment for yourself, and see if it doesn't make keeping healthy easier and more fun. Used in conjunction with a healthy balanced diet and exercise, the results are sure to please you.

Chapter 16

THE POWER AND THE SPIRIT

Opposites are merely two sides of the same coin.

The evolution revolution is speeding up in the 1990s; it's flowing and unfolding everywhere at once. The phenomenon was not instigated by humans, although individuals can be consciously aware of the growing process. The One Source of the universe is evolving and this growth is reflected in galaxies, stars, solar systems, planets and everything that makes up a planetary being.

Many entities live together as a planetary being. Spirits, minerals, plants, fish, birds, insects, animals, humans, air, water, earth. These, and many other elements, compose the complex planetary consciousness with its many aspects of one being.

We live with the other aspects of our planetary being independently and also interdependently. Does this mean we're one and *not* one at the same time? No, we're always one. Only humans appear to have the option to think, feel or imagine they are not one with all. This is an illusion of the human mind.

As we humans become more aware of ourselves, we become more aware of everything else. What do we do about that? Love!

Love it all—the perception, the experience, the process and the flow of life.

Are we ready to express unconditional love on this planet Earth? Yes. We need the most powerful force in the universe to heal our world.

Remember the old mercenary saying? "Kill them all; let God sort them out." With unconditional love, we'd change it to, "Love them all; let God sort them out." This is a change of attitude on Earth that is creating a happier, more peaceful world. The attitude of unconditional love expresses a reverence for all life, even more, for all of creation.

Can this be lived each day or is it just for philosophical debates and religious gatherings? It can be lived each day, if people develop a conscious awareness of themselves and the world around them. This conscious awareness leads to the realization of the connectedness of the individual to his or her world. More awareness creates a more beautiful world.

Individual people have a tremendous effect on the mass human consciousness that creates the world around us. The beneficial effect happens right now. Now is the only time it can happen. The future isn't here yet and the past has gone by, so now is the time for peaceful loving change. This process of growth takes place inside the hearts and minds of people. It radiates outward to others through the human spirit. Two ways that we can promote unconditional love and the expansion of mass consciousness are through the pipe ceremony and individual healing.

HEALING CIRCLE—THE PIPE CEREMONY

The healing circle opens with a crystal pipe prayer ceremony and a circle of people. We've outlined below one version of the pipe ceremony done with the crystal pipe described in the book *Crystal Spirit*:

The participants of the pipe ceremony sit or stand in a circle with spiritual objects at its center (i.e., crystals, feathers, shells and other items that hold spiritual significance for the group).

The leader of the ceremony says, "We make an offering for the spirit people," and uses a crystal or crystal light rod to circle the pipe's crystal bowl in a clockwise direction one to three times. The words and the circling motion are repeated for mineral people, plant people, people of the sea, winged people, four-legged brothers and sisters, two-legged brothers and sisters, Sky Father/Mother and Earth Mother/Father.

Next the leader rotates the stem of the pipe clockwise until the stem crystal points to the east, and says, "I call upon the wind of wisdom from the east to come into our circle." Then the pipe is rotated the rest of the way around until the stem crystal is pointing towards the leader's mouth. He or she breathes the breath of life by exhaling into the stem crystal of the pipe while imagining the exhalation flowing outward through the universe, then inhaling and imagining the breath streaming back through the pipe.

The pipe is next rotated to the south and the leader says, "I call upon the wind of growth from the south to come into our circle." The stem is rotated back to the mouth once again and the breath of life repeated. The whole process is repeated twice more—once for the "wind of regeneration from the west" and once for the "wind of purity from the north."

After the last breath of life for the north, the pipe stem is rotated clockwise until it points straight over the leader's head and he or she says, "We offer this to the Great Spirit." The pipe is brought down in clockwise motion and the breath of life is repeated. Then the stem is rotated until it points to the ground and the words "We offer this to the Earth Mother/Father" are spoken. The pipe stem is rotated back to the mouth and the breath of life is done. Finally the pipe is rotated so the bowl is in the right hand and the stem is in the left hand held straight out from the chest, then the pipe is carefully laid on the earth.

This completes the basic ceremony which can be followed by a joining of hands when each person in the circle has an opportunity to speak their words for healing in a clockwise order. When everyone who wishes to has spoken, the circle closes in as the participants join arm in arm and the leader directs anyone who wishes to silently send healing energy to friends, family and anyone else who may need it. After a few minutes, the leader says, "The visualized heartfelt sphere of good energy in this circle is expanding and growing outward to encompass the whole planet then radiating outward through the universe." There is a period of silent meditation. When sufficient time has passed, the leader closes by saying, "We give thanks for this circle, all the good things experienced, and our brothers and sisters. Thanks is given for our guidance on the path that led us here now and for guidance on the path to come." The participants then exchange hugs with each other.

Once the first, formal, part of the ceremony is finished, the last half varies according to the individuals present and the needs of the participants. But if you wish to conduct a pipe ceremony of your own, the above gives you a good basic format to start with. Remember that the most important element of the circle is the healing engendered by the spirit of the participants working together for this purpose.

SPIRITUAL HEALING

The healing circle is often followed by a spiritual healing in which the life, universal, *ki* or *chi* energy is used for individual healing. To do this, first form a ball, or sun, of energy by cupping and shaping it with the hands. The hands are held a few inches apart in cupped position. There will be a tingling in the palms as the energy builds and grows. Rotate the palms around this ball of energy for a few moments.

When the energy feels as if it's too great to be contained by the cupped hands, healing energy can be sent to another person without physically touching the person. This is done by holding both hands close together, palms downward, a few inches from the area of the person's body that needs healing. The energy pouring from the hands usually causes a tingling sensation. When the energy is flowing to an afflicted, out-of-balance, area the sensations of warmth and heat are felt. The feeling of heat usually turns cool or neutral after three to ten minutes. This is a sign that the area has received enough energy to balance the natural energy channels in the body in most cases. Flick the fingers or shake the hands when the healing is done to dissipate the energy.

The healing process described, as with most spiritual practices, is a general guide for the way it works for most people, but not all. It is always best to follow your own intuition and sensory feedback impressions to determine what works for your personally.

The process for a healing in which the specific out-of-balance area is not known is very similar to the one above. After building the sun of energy between your palms the hands are held a few inches away from the body and moved slowly over the body until a warm afflicted area is felt. After that, the hands are held over that area until it cools. The head and heart areas are a good place for healing, if no hot areas can be found.

To do an individual healing with a crystal or a crystal rod, hold the rod or crystal in one hand (experiment to see which one feels best) and cup the other hand over, but not touching, the point of the crystal to build your sun of energy. After that, the hand and the rod are used together the same way as two hands can be used. We advise trying both methods of healing, with and without a crystal, so that you can compare the difference in energy to see what works best for you in any particular circumstance. Chances are that sometimes one method will feel better and sometimes the other, so it's good to have both ways at your disposal when you need them.

The head and heart areas are a good place to start the healing process, even if the affliction is already known. The reason for this is that many kinds of disease result from thoughts (head) and emotions (heart) that cause energy imbalances or blockages in other areas of the body. Relief can quite often be achieved by directing the healing energy to one or both of these sources. These are also areas that need to be balanced in the crystal warrior for the expression of unconditional love.

The warrior and healer are two sides of the same coin, one and connected. The universal energy of spirit is the same energy used by both the warrior and the healer or the warrior/healer as one balanced entity. They both act with an awareness of the inner world of spirit. This is the world beyond thoughts and emotions. This is the world of balanced flowing energy. The warrior with the crystal sword is the same person as the healer with the crystal healing rod. The warrior/healer is the energy circuit that transforms and moves energy from one world to another, spiritual to physical, with the conscious awareness of the one energy that connects and creates both worlds as one.

FINAL WORDS

People often ask why there are so many different kinds of crystal tools and devices in *Crystal Power* and *Crystal Spirit*? The reason is that every crystal tool of growth isn't right for everybody. By providing a variety of tools, it's possible for each person, no matter what type of background or interests, to find one that suits him or her. We also encourage people to change and modify any and all of these according to their intuition and feelings of what is right for them. There are as many paths to spiritual growth as there are people, and all of them are "right." The most important part of any of these tools is the individual human spirit and consciousness; the crystals and the tools are secondary support for spiritual growth and awareness.

Many people also wonder why it's necessary to provide crystal tools in the form of guns. The reaction to these guns, in some cases, is emphatic and extreme because up to this time guns have always been a symbol of violence. If you experience this kind of reaction, it may be due to a part of you that has been repressed and needs to be looked at in a calm dispassionate manner. A good way to do this is to build a crystal gun that is to be used for healing rather than destruction.

The simple truth is that guns are a part of our society and are probably here to stay. As has been shown with prohibition, drug repression and civil rights, legislation isn't effective in eliminating undesirable elements or attitudes. What is effective is the growth of the individual to a point beyond where these elements are necessary in order for them to feel good or safe.

At the present time, to many people, a gun is a symbol of personal power and freedom. People who don't feel in control of their environment or themselves need this kind of symbol. Take away the gun symbol, assuming it could be done, and another will replace it because the need will still be there waiting to be filled. The practical solution is to use the symbol the gun represents to help us grow beyond a feeling of powerlessness—to experience our own power and magnificence.

Once we begin associating with crystals it's impossible not to grow and learn. For when we embark on the crystal path of growth, no return is possible. The person who is not ready for growth will either not be attracted by crystals or will find them extremely uncomfortable to be around. No one knows how or why they promote growth, but the fact is that they do. Using the crystals in conjunction with objects a person is already interested in may create a motivation to experience crystals that wouldn't be there otherwise. Imagine for a moment what a wonderful world ours would be if all guns were converted to crystal tools of light and learning, and you'll understand why they were created.

The same could be said for crystal knives, staffs, swords and martial arts equipment. They were created because they're tools we're familiar with and can relate to. All these items are now being used by people for spiritual and physical development. The use of these tools usually involves prayers, meditation and an attitude of reverence while practicing the various styles and techniques these are applied to. Crystals enhance and amplify these positive uses even more.

Crystal Warrior is intended to provide a wide variety of crystal tools and spiritual experiences. Many of these have been asked for by the readers of *Crystal Power* and *Crystal Spirit*. As unique individuals, we're able to make personal choices about what we need for our own development. We require many different kinds of growth experiences. Many people may read this book and build some of the crystal tools in it, but each person's experiences with these tools will be unique and will add to the effort we're all making to create a world of love and harmony.

CHANNELED MESSAGE

The 1990s, the last decade of the century, has inspired the creation of many new tools of spiritual growth for the crystal warrior. The "Decade of the Crystal" has also given us many messages of hope and love. We conclude with a message channeled by one of the authors:

The 1990s will bring about massive changes and expansion in human consciousness. This will be a time when spiritual forces coalesce and converge to form the new ideas that will transform your world in the coming century. These changes will take time to complete, but they are speeding up at what may seem to be an alarming pace to many of you.

Change is not to be feared. Although it may be disruptive, you will soon perceive that it was necessary for your own personal growth. Growth that will enable you to embrace a world where love, harmony and cooperation predominate.

If, during this time of change, you feel out of balance and disorganized, even depressed, please focus on the positive elements in your lives. Do not be afraid. All is well and will continue to be well. Glory in each new day for the wonders it brings and look to small moments of beauty and love for strength. Use those resources that are within each of you, and the tools that are given for your use to rise to new heights.

—David

The adventure of crystals, magic and shamanism is like the circle of life itself. You can begin anywhere and there is no end to the unlimited varieties of conscious awareness and creative experiences. The *Crystal Power, Crystal Spirit, Crystal Warrior* trilogy seeks to share these experiences with all our brothers and sisters in a spirit of unconditional love. We've tried to keep our minds open to the unlimited possibilities for new experiences of personal and universal growth. We share them with you so that we can all make the most of our lives together on Earth.

Appendix A

NEW RODS FOR THE NINETIES

Crystal tools during the Earth's evolution provide humans for generations to come with the means for transformation and revolution.

Many of the tools for the 1990s that have been given to us are described in this chapter. The rods all work with universal energy, directed by mind and emotion, using the same basic construction techniques. The shapes and forms are different, but the principles are the same. Use these rods for healing, meditation, martial arts—whatever your individual spirit says you must do with them.

WOODEN CRYSTAL RODS

Crystal rods with wooden handgrips are becoming popular with crystal enthusiasts because of their unique beauty and feel. Another reason for the popularity of wooden crystal rods, is that some people don't want to use animal hides to cover their crystal rods. While other alternatives are available, such as plastic electrical tape,

PVC shrink tubing or even leaving the copper tube uncovered, the most aesthetically pleasing way is to use wood that doesn't need a covering.

These rods require a piece of wood 6" or longer, depending on your personal preference. Most types of wood (hard or soft) can be bought or cut into 3/4" square pieces. Lengths of 6" are almost a minimum since the copper couplers on each end or a coupler and a copper cap each take up 1/2". When these are applied, the wooden handgrip becomes 1" shorter, leaving 5" for the center.

SINGLE AND DOUBLE WOODEN RODS

Materials:

Double Rod

  A. Two quartz crystals, 1-1/4" diameter by 1-1/2" length

  B. Two 1/2" copper couplings

  C. 6" length of wood, 3/4" square or round

  D. Lacquer, stain or oil finish for wood

Single Rod

  A. One quartz crystal, 1-1/4" diameter by 1-1/2" length

  B. 1/2" copper coupling

  C. 6" length of wood, 3/4" square or round

  D. 1/2" diameter copper end cap

  E. Lacquer, stain or oil finish for wood

Construction:

Shaping the Wood

The hardest part about building these rods is shaping the wood. The 3/4" square by 6" length of wood should be rounded slightly for a comfortable handgrip. It also must be rounded to a 1/2" diameter, 1/2" from either end of the wood as is shown in the diagram, so it will fit into the copper coupler or end cap. This is no problem if you have a wood lathe, but since most of us don't unless we are serious woodworkers, we've come up with other ways to shape the wood using inexpensive tools like a power drill with a grinding wheel attachment, a small finish sander, a rasp and a piece of sandpaper for final touch-up work.

The grinding wheel and the sander both are needed for shaping hardwoods, while the sander is usually enough for the softwoods. If you're lucky enough to be able to find the kind of wood you want in a rounded shape, so much the better. Each type of wood has advantages and disadvantages. The hardwoods are generally more attractive and can be hand-rubbed with only a coat of lemon oil, but they are more expensive to buy and harder to work with. The softwoods, on the other hand, are cheap and easy to work with, but are less durable and may need a stain and/or a finish coat to beautify and protect them. Either way, it's going to take some work to shape them, but the finished article can be a beautiful work of art well worth having and using.

Assembly

To assemble the rod, follow the specifications on the diagram. The quartz crystals are mounted into 1/2" diameter copper couplings using copper screen or copper foil (which is available at stained glass stores) wrapped around the end of the crystal to be fitted and an instant bonding glue to secure it. The double crystal rod requires two crystals of slightly less than 1/2" diameter to be fit into couplings, while the single crystal rod only needs one. A 1/2" copper cap will replace the crystal on the other end of the single rod. Instant bonding glue works well to attach both the crystal in the coupling and the copper end cap to the center wooden handgrip.

It's advisable to apply the lemon oil or stain (depending on whether you use hard- or softwood) after the rod has been glued together. The reason for this is that the glue may not adhere properly to some wood treatments or finishes.

Other Ideas

To make a more finished looking rod, polish the copper couplings and caps. You can do this by hand using a copper cleaner or in a rock tumbler with jeweler's rouge. If you want your rod to maintain it's bright finish without tarnishing after it is built, a lacquer can be sprayed on the couplings before the crystals are mounted.

Improvisations can be just as fun and exciting on wooden crystal rods as on the other types of crystal rods. Feathers, beadwork and gemstones can be added to these rods to make them a beautiful personalized work or they can be left just as they are for a smoother feel. One inch square lengths of wood can be crafted to take three-quarter inch diameter copper couplings for a heftier rod. Of course longer lengths of wood can be used for either size.

As with other crystal rods, the variations you can come up with to make your rod something that is uniquely yours are endless. Build your rod with a sense of fun and adventure that lets you employ any variation that pleases you and you will enjoy it all that much more when it's done.

WOODEN CRYSTAL RODS

DOUBLE ROD WITH WOODEN HANDGRIP

QUARTZ CRYSTAL | ½" COPPER COUPLING | 6" LENGTH WOOD ¾" SQ. | ½" COPPER COUPLING | QUARTZ CRYSTAL

WOOD ½" X ½" LENGTH & DIAMETER | 5" WOOD SLIGHTLY ROUNDED | WOOD ½" X ½" LENGTH & DIAMETER

FINISHED ROD

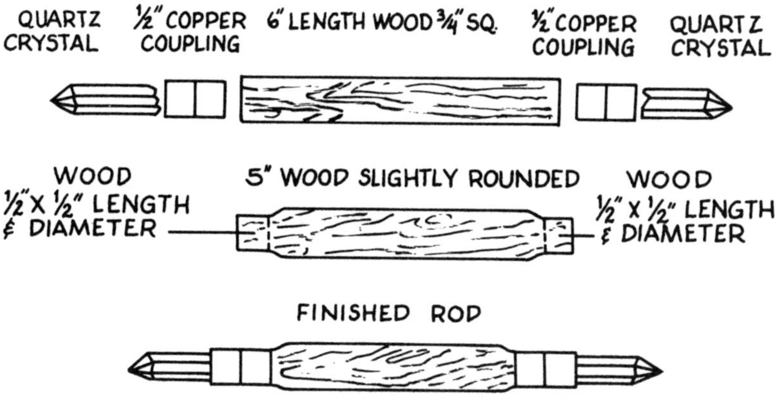

SINGLE ROD WITH WOODEN HANDGRIP

½" COPPER CAP | 6" LENGTH WOOD ¾" SQ. | ½" COPPER COUPLING | QUARTZ CRYSTAL

WOOD ½" X ½" LENGTH & DIAMETER | 5" WOOD SLIGHTLY ROUNDED | WOOD ½" X ½" LENGTH & DIAMETER

FINISHED ROD

CRYSTAL SPIKE RODS

Crystal spike rods are made with long thin crystals, beautiful to look at, but also good for directing universal spiritual energy. One other aspect of these crystals is that they resemble stilettos. It's all in the eye of the beholder. Crystal spike rods could be used as an effective martial arts-type defense stick, but chances are that by the time you've progressed this far in your use of crystals, your defenses will be inner-directed and spiritual in nature. "The greatest healer can be the greatest warrior and the greatest warrior can be the greatest healer."

Crystal spike rods are named for the shape of the crystals used in them. These are quartz crystals, 3-1/2 to 4" long, tapered slightly to a small sharp pointed tip. They are not more than 1/2" in diameter at the widest part of their base.

The total overall length of these rods varies according to the length of the crystals. The short ones use two crystals and are about 7-1/2 to 8" in length. The longer ones, using three crystals, are approximately 11 to 12" long. The diagrams have measurements as a general guide only, since lengths of quartz crystals are seldom the same for any two or three that might be used.

Materials:

A. Quartz crystal 1-1/2" length, 1/2" diameter

B. Two 1/2" copper couplings

C. 2" length of 1/2" copper tubing

D. Quartz crystal, thin spike shape, 3-1/2" to 4" long

E. 3-1/4" length of 1/2" copper tubing

F. Leather strip 1/2" wide, long enough to cover tubing

G. Copper mesh or copper foil tape, 1/2" wide for wrapping and mounting crystals

H. Instant bonding glue

I. 1/2" copper end cap

Construction:

The center copper coupling is the key to these rods, since it forms the joint where the rods can be put together or taken apart as desired. The crystal is mounted, like other rods, by wrapping copper mesh or copper tape around the bottom 1/2" at the widest part of the base. The crystal is turned as it's pushed into the copper coupling. Unlike the other rods, where the mounting material is glued so it's even with the end of the coupling, this one is pushed down inside the coupling until the mounting around the crystal is recessed at least 1/4" or more from the open end of the coupling. This allows the 1/4" of exposed copper tubing on the other part of the rod to slide in and out of this coupling when putting the rods together as one or taking them apart to have two rods in one. The rod uses 1/2" diameter copper tubing, although the same pattern could be used with larger diameter crystals and copper tubing easily.

The crystals can be mounted and glued right away, but none of the other parts should be glued until they've been fitted together several times to see if they need adjustments before final gluing and leather wrap. Remember not to glue the center coupling where it's supposed to slide in and out of the top copper tube.

TRIPLE CRYSTAL SPIKE ROD

The triple crystal spike rod, when put together, can be used as a double-ended rod. When the two halves of this rod are taken apart, there is one single crystal rod and one double. The two halves can be used in both hands or one of them can be loaned to a friend for martial arts practice, healing or directing energy.

Materials:

A. Three spike-shaped quartz crystals 3-1/2" to 4" long with bases slightly less than 1/2" diameter

B. Copper mesh or copper foil tape, 1/2" wide for wrapping and mounting crystals

C. Instant bonding glue

D. Three 1/2" copper couplings

E. 2-1/4" length of 1/2" copper tubing

F. 4-1/4" length of 1/2" copper tubing

G. 1/2" wide leather strips long enough to wrap both sections

Construction:

This variation of the spike rod is constructed the same as the double crystal spike rod except a third crystal mounted in a coupling replaces the copper end cap (see diagram). The handgrip with two crystals can also be made longer if desired.

Other Variations

These rods can also be made leaving all or some of the copper couplings uncovered, wrapping the leather so that only half of the couplings are covered or covering the couplings completely with leather. You may use shorter or longer quartz crystals depending on your personal preference.

CRYSTAL SPIKE RODS

DOUBLE CRYSTAL SPIKE ROD

2" LONG COPPER TUBING

COPPER COUPLING WITH RECESSED CRYSTAL MOUNTING

COPPER COUPLING LEATHER WRAPPED

¼" EXPOSED TUBING

3¼" LONG COPPER TUBING

COPPER END CAP

TRIPLE CRYSTAL SPIKE ROD

2¼" LONG COPPER TUBING

COPPER COUPLING WITH RECESSED CRYSTAL MOUNTING

COPPER COUPLING

¼" EXPOSED TUBING

4½" LONG COPPER TUBING

COPPER COUPLING

CONTAINER CRYSTAL ROD WITH HANDGUARD

The container rod has a handguard that resembles some Eastern and martial arts-type sword guards. It can be used as a martial arts tool, using the *ki* and *chi* energy to achieve harmony by bringing order out of chaos. This rod can be made even more like a self-defense tool by placing one of the triangular tipped steel or space age plastic self-defense spikes inside the hollow copper tube. Ancient knowledge says we should be able to sense where trouble or a potentially dangerous learning situation might be and simply *not be there!* If, once in a great while, this doesn't quite work, it's comforting to have back-up reserves. This approach was used by most of the ancient teachers. The corollary to this in our own society might be, "never put all your eggs in one basket." Ancient teachers were (and still are) practical and down-to-earth.

Materials:

A. Three 1/2" copper couplings

B. Two 4-1/4" lengths of 1/2" copper tubing

C. One 3/4" length of 1/2" copper tubing

D. One quartz crystal 1-1/2" to 2" length, 1/2" diameter

E. Copper mesh or copper foil tape, 1/2" wide for wrapping and mounting crystal

F. Instant bonding glue

G. 1/2" copper end cap

H. Concho or coin for handguard 1-1/2" to 2-1/4" diameter, can be brass, copper, silver or bronze

I. Two strips of leather 1/2" wide, long enough to wrap each section

Construction:

The top half of this rod is composed of one, 4-1/2" length of 1/2" copper tubing; three 1/2" copper couplings (one for the crystal mounting and two as the center joint connection and handguard holder). The handguard is made by drilling a 1/2" diameter hole in a brass concho. A coin can also be used as a handguard. A 3/4" long piece of 1/2" diameter copper tubing is glued to join the two center copper couplings with the handguard. Then, a 1-1/2 to 2" long quartz crystal with a diameter slightly less than 1/2" is mounted in a 1/2" copper coupling. This is done by wrapping the bottom part of the crystal in copper mesh or copper tape to achieve a tight fit and then gluing the wrapped portion of the crystal into the coupling with instant bonding glue. The mounted crystal is then glued onto the end of the long tube. A 1/2" wide piece of leather is used to wrap the rod below the crystal to the handguard, gluing it as you wrap.

The bottom half of of the device is used as a handgrip. It is composed of the other 4-1/2" length of 1/2" diameter copper tubing glued to the 1/2" diameter copper cap. The bottom half of the rod is then wrapped with leather from the end cap to the opposite end leaving 1/2" of copper tube exposed so that it will fit inside the copper coupling in the top half behind the handguard.

Other Uses

The hollow center is an excellent place to keep healing stones of all kinds. The container in this rod may also be used to store important papers, maps, money or other items. Its uses are endless and varied, according to your inclination.

EXTENSION RODS

If you'd like a fairly compact rod that can be lengthened when necessary, then the extension rod is the one for you to build.

Materials:

A. 1-1/2" to 2" long quartz crystal 1/2" in diameter

B. Copper mesh or copper foil tape, 1/2" wide for wrapping and mounting crystal

C. Instant bonding glue

D. 1/2" copper coupling

E. 7" length of 1/2" diameter brass tubing

F. 7" length of brass tubing one size smaller than 1/2" diameter

G. 1/2" copper end cap

H. Leather strip 1/2" wide, long enough to wrap 7" length of 1/2" diameter brass tubing

Construction:

This rod uses two 7" lengths of brass tubing (available at most hobby shops) instead of the usual copper tubing. One length is 1/2" in diameter, while the other length is just slightly smaller in diameter. This lets one length of brass tubing slide in and out of the other length. This rod works the same way as an extendible radio antenna, except it's just two sections of equal length instead of four to six. (Smaller versions of this rod can also be constructed using short, small diameter radio antennas.)

The crystal is less than 1/2" in diameter and 1-1/2 to 2" long. It's mounted in the 1/2" copper coupling using a wrapped shim of copper mesh or copper tape adhered with instant bonding glue. This is, in turn, glued on one end of the smaller diameter brass tubing. A 1/2" copper cap is glued on the end of the larger brass rod and then the brass portion is wrapped with leather.

Comments:

Nothing in our universe is inherently "good" or "bad." That's a matter of personal interpretation. Our universe and our real inner selves actually only seek "the balance." Enjoyment and growth can be experienced by creating any crystal tool that pleases you.

CRYSTAL CONTAINER ROD

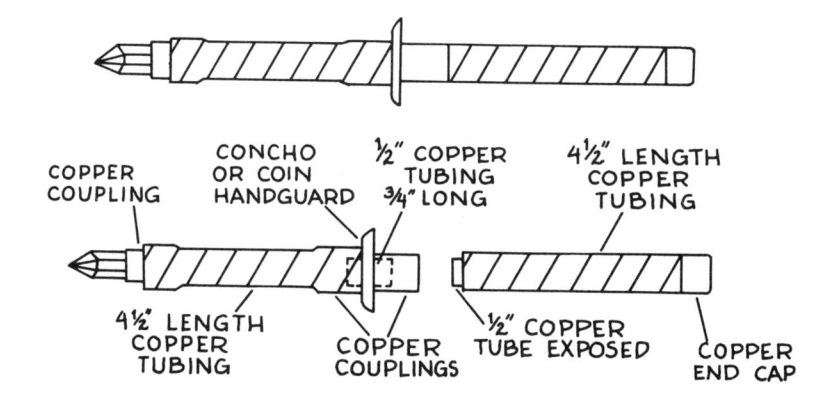

- COPPER COUPLING
- CONCHO OR COIN HANDGUARD
- ½" COPPER TUBING ¾" LONG
- 4½" LENGTH COPPER TUBING
- 4½" LENGTH COPPER TUBING
- COPPER COUPLINGS
- ½" COPPER TUBE EXPOSED
- COPPER END CAP

CRYSTAL EXTENSION ROD

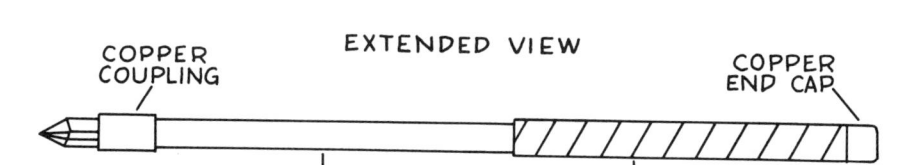

EXTENDED VIEW

- COPPER COUPLING
- COPPER END CAP
- 7" BRASS TUBE
- 7" BRASS TUBE LEATHER WRAPPED

CRYSTAL SQUEEZE AND PENLIGHT RODS

The crystal squeeze and penlight rods can be among the most exciting crystal devices to build and use. They are fairly inexpensive, easy to build and they can be assembled without the use of tools that may be necessary to complete some of the more complicated crystal projects.

Another advantage of lighted crystal rods is that they allow us to see deep down into the interior worlds of crystals. We can see galaxies, pyramids, pathways, plateaus and doorways that we might miss otherwise. A lighted crystal is a thing of beauty, but it also intensifies the crystal's energy and can provide a new learning-growing life experience.

These crystal light rods are made with so-called disposable flashlights. However, these flashlights need not be disposed of when the batteries wear out. The flashlights can all be cut with a tubing cutter or pried apart with a pocket or kitchen knife. The batteries and bulbs can be replaced and the flashlights taped back together. Most can also be cut with a razor knife to replace batteries and/or bulbs at much lower than the original cost.

Comments:

Our government and our products are a direct reflection of our culture and ourselves. Now, we may all be replaceable, we hope we are fixable; but who wants to be disposable? That's why we like to fix disposable products. Another issue is that of waste; it goes against the grain. We feel that it's necessary in our day and age to make the best use of the products our technology is able to supply us without being wasteful. We don't want to see our society become a disposable, throw-away item any more than we want to become disposable ourselves.

Materials:

A. Quartz crystal to fit light

B. Silver foil tape

C. Copper foil tape

D. Copper coupling, 1/2" (optional mounting)

E. Squeezelight or penlight

Construction:

All light rods can be made easily and economically by using silver foil tape (available at most hardware stores) and copper foil tape (available where stained glass supplies are sold).

Before you attach the crystal, it's a good idea to test it with a lighted flashlight since some crystals reflect and radiate light much better than others.

The next step is to wrap and attach the crystals to the flashlights with silver foil tape. The silver tape will increase the light reflection through the quartz crystals. The copper foil tape can then be wrapped over the silver and all down the length of the flashlight for a nice-looking finish. In just a few minutes you can have a finished crystal light rod.

This kind of construction is adaptable to all sizes and types of flashlights. It's easy to experiment and improve on the original design.

In making these lighted rods, one thing to keep in mind is that the light and heat interact with the molecules in the crystals exciting them and causing them to emit energy more powerfully than they do when they are in a cold state. This can make your light rod a very powerful tool for directing energy and promoting spiritual growth in a world that has desperate need of it both on an individual and global scale.

SQUEEZE & PENLIGHT RODS

SQUEEZELIGHT ROD

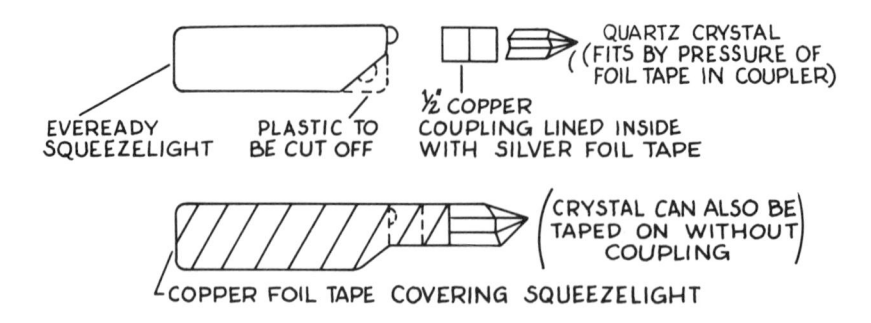

EVEREADY SQUEEZELIGHT — PLASTIC TO BE CUT OFF

½ COPPER COUPLING LINED INSIDE WITH SILVER FOIL TAPE

QUARTZ CRYSTAL (FITS BY PRESSURE OF FOIL TAPE IN COUPLER)

COPPER FOIL TAPE COVERING SQUEEZELIGHT

(CRYSTAL CAN ALSO BE TAPED ON WITHOUT COUPLING)

DISPOSABLE PENLIGHT RODS

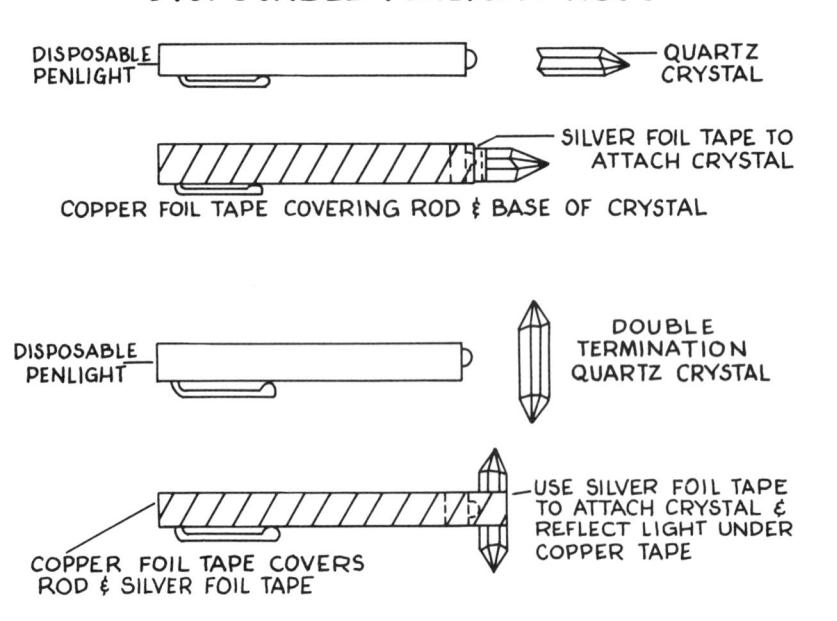

DISPOSABLE PENLIGHT

QUARTZ CRYSTAL

COPPER FOIL TAPE COVERING ROD & BASE OF CRYSTAL

SILVER FOIL TAPE TO ATTACH CRYSTAL

DISPOSABLE PENLIGHT

DOUBLE TERMINATION QUARTZ CRYSTAL

COPPER FOIL TAPE COVERS ROD & SILVER FOIL TAPE

USE SILVER FOIL TAPE TO ATTACH CRYSTAL & REFLECT LIGHT UNDER COPPER TAPE

Appendix B

PIEZO RODS AND CRYSTAL FRIVOLITIES

If primitive people needed psi talents to survive and grow and the talents went dormant when our civilized technological society developed, why are these talents coming back to people now?

PIEZO CRYSTAL RODS

Piezo crystal rods, in essence, use a crystalline substance to produce a spark that will excite the atoms in a quartz crystal. The effect is similar but not exactly like that of the crystal light rods. You'll find experimenting with this unique blend of light and heat energies an interesting process.

There are a variety of piezo lighters on the market today that will produce sparks for lighting furnaces, barbecues, campfires, etc. They are readily available in many stores. Two types are listed below and the methods of constructing them.

The piezo flash can best be seen through the crystal in dark or dim light conditions. Before mounting the crystal, turn it to see what position produces the most dramatic flash. When the brightest position is found, the crystal can be permanently mounted on the particular piezo crystal rod you are constructing.

LEIFHEIT MODEL

Materials:

A. Leifheit (brand name) piezo lighter

B. Silver foil tape

C. Copper foil tape

D. Copper coupling, 1/2" (optional)

E. Quartz crystal

Construction:

The best piezo lighter is probably the German, Leifheit model, which can be found where camping supplies are sold. This lighter produces the biggest spark with the least effort. The rod can be built two different ways. The easiest way is to tape the quartz crystal to the end of the lighter with silver foil tape and then cover the silver foil tape with copper tape about a third the length of the igniter.

The second method is more difficult, but produces a more finished looking product and is a more durable mounting for the crystal. For this rod, the crystal is pressure-fitted into a silver foil-lined 1/2" copper coupling. The coupling is then taped onto the piezo lighter with copper foil tape. Copper foil tape can be used to cover any part, or all, of the plastic body of the piezo lighter.

With either of the above methods of construction, the piezo lighters could also be wrapped with leather so as to look more like the traditional crystal rods.

PIEZO IGNITER CRYSTAL ROD

Materials:

A. Piezo igniter for gas grill or furnace

B. Flat metal washer to fit spark end of igniter, less than 1" outside diameter (may need to grind down)

C. Copper tubing 3-1/2" long by 1" diameter

D. Copper end cap for 1" tubing

E. Silver foil tape

F. Quartz crystal to fit 1" tubing

G. Copper foil tape

H. Instant bonding glue

Construction:

The second type of piezo rod is made with the type of igniters used in gas barbecues and furnaces and requires some assembly before it's functional. To construct this model, slide the washer on the spark end of the igniter. Later, the igniter will be mounted in the 3" length of copper tubing with a copper end cap. The cap needs to have a hole drilled in it for mounting the push-button switch assembly. The quartz crystal is wrapped with silver foil tape to enhance light reflection. After that, the crystal is wrapped with copper foil tape or copper mesh so it will fit the copper tube securely before it is glued in place with instant bonding glue. The piezo igniter is then pushed into the copper tube and the end cap is glued on. Before you glue the end cap, test the switch to make sure it's working properly.

Why Build a Piezo Crystal Rod?

We found the idea of using a piezo crystal lighter to produce miniature lightning in and around natural quartz crystals an intriguing idea. Some people use the piezo igniters on the acupressure points of the body for healing. The addition of a natural quartz crystal, which is also good for healing, adds a double energy benefit in this area.

The concept of producing a visible effect in an area where most of the energy we work with is invisible, except to some psychics, also attracted our interest. We hope you'll find these useful, enjoyable and entertaining crystal inventions.

PIEZO CRYSTAL RODS

(LEIFHEIT) PIEZO CRYSTAL ROD

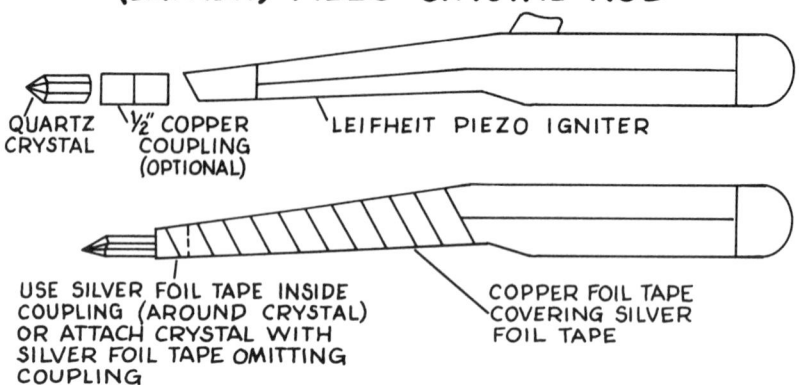

QUARTZ CRYSTAL
½" COPPER COUPLING (OPTIONAL)
LEIFHEIT PIEZO IGNITER

USE SILVER FOIL TAPE INSIDE COUPLING (AROUND CRYSTAL) OR ATTACH CRYSTAL WITH SILVER FOIL TAPE OMITTING COUPLING

COPPER FOIL TAPE COVERING SILVER FOIL TAPE

PIEZO IGNITER CRYSTAL ROD

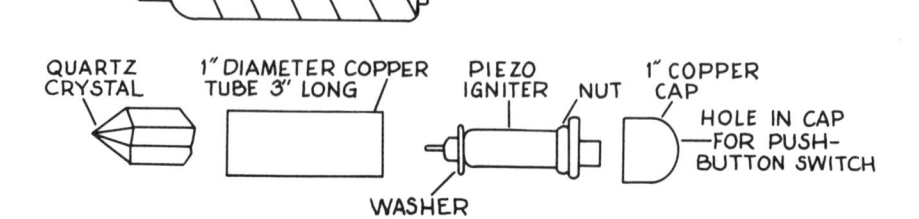

QUARTZ CRYSTAL
1" DIAMETER COPPER TUBE 3" LONG
PIEZO IGNITER
NUT
1" COPPER CAP
HOLE IN CAP FOR PUSH-BUTTON SWITCH
WASHER

CRYSTAL FRIVOLITIES

As in many other areas, with crystals it's easy to become too tight instead of light. By that we mean that we have a tendency to take ourselves too seriously.

The One Source plays with the energies of the universe in creating interacting forms of infinite variety. Everything from new galaxies and planets to new species of plants and animals, even new mineral combinations is brought or thought into being for the experience of the pure joy of creation and being. That's playing for the sheer fun of it. We, as human beings, can learn from the Source's example to lighten up and live more fully with the same playful spirit of creation.

Unusual Crystal Tools

It's ironic that these crystal devices appear unusual because they're so ordinary. Most of the crystal tools we use are considered dramatic or exotic at first, then they become ordinary after years of use. This section deals with ordinary tools that become more interesting because quartz crystals have been added to them.

The other difference in these tools is that they don't have to do anything other than what they were intended for. They just do their same jobs with quartz crystals attached. The quartz crystals also just do their job. They connect into and radiate energy through the energy web of the Earth and the energy matrix of the universe at the same time. They're also pretty to look at as they turn an ordinary item into a work of art.

These tools don't have to do anything else, but they can if you desire them to. Other people may be a bit surprised if you use a crystal comb or toothbrush as a healing rod, but they certainly will work for that. Where there's a crystal, there's healing, balancing energy. It just looks unusual to see a healing cane or umbrella, that's all. It's even more strange to see a crystal riding crop or crystal bullwhip, but they make fine decorative items for your home.

The crystal razor is another ordinary everyday tool. We don't know if a crystal razor will help you get a closer shave, but it does add beauty and energy to an everyday task.

Almost everybody uses a pen for writing at least once a day, so attaching a crystal to a ballpoint pen is a great idea. It can be put on anything from a gold Cross pen to a plastic Bic pen. The result is the same. You have a beautiful energetic crystal to look at while using your pen.

Another tool similar in size and shape to the pen is the extension pointer that some people use when giving a talk or lecture. A crystal on its pointing tip changes this mundane article into something else altogether. Crystals can even be attached to both ends of this pocket-size, pen-shaped device if you desire.

CRYSTAL PENS, POINTERS, RAZORS, COMBS AND TOOTHBRUSHES

Materials:

  A. Small quartz crystal 1/2"–3/4" long by 1/4" diameter

  B. Silver foil tape 1" wide by 2" long

  C. Copper foil tape, 3/8" to 1/2" wide and 6"–8" long

  D. Cross pen, extension pointer, razor, comb or toothbrush of any type

Construction:

The same easy method is used to attach crystals to each of these five tools. Silver foil tape is used first to connect the crystal to the end of the tool. This tape has thicker stronger glue than the copper tape and its silver surface allows the crystal to reflect light so that it retains its natural clear appearance. The strip of copper foil tape is tightly wrapped in a spiral pattern over the silver tape and part of the tool being worked on, as far down as you like. The copper tape provides an extra secure attachment and it looks nice on the crystal tool. One advantage to these devices is that they're easy and economical to build.

This is a guideline for working with crystals in a new way and a new direction. Look around and see what other everyday items around the home or office you can enhance with crystals.

CRYSTAL FRIVOLITIES

THE CRYSTAL CROSS PEN

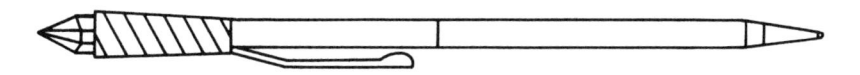

THE CRYSTAL POINTER

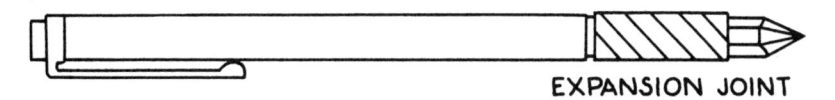

EXPANSION JOINT

THE CRYSTAL RAZOR

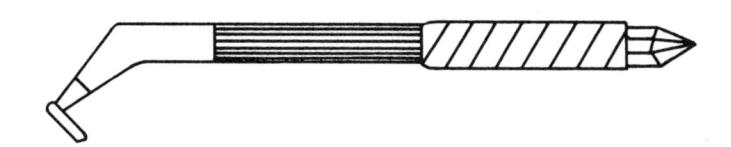

THE CRYSTAL COMB

THE CRYSTAL TOOTHBRUSH

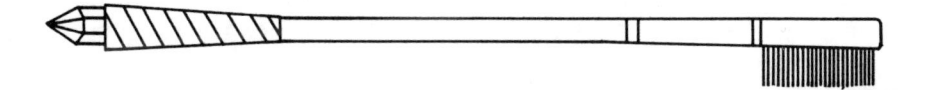

CRYSTAL UMBRELLA

Another common everyday item that can be transformed into a crystal delight is the umbrella. There's nothing better for keeping dry, but be careful not to rest its crystal point on the ground for fear of damaging your crystal.

Materials:

Handle End Attachment

  A. Quartz crystal, 2" long by 3/4" diameter

  B. 1/2" wide strip copper foil tape as long as needed

  C. 3/4" copper coupling

  D. Instant bonding glue

  E. Standard-sized umbrella

  F. Leather wrap as needed 3/4" wide

Pointed End Attachment

  A. Copper tubing, 5" long by 1/2" diameter

  B. Quartz crystal 1" long by slightly less than 1/2" diameter

  C. Copper tape for shim on crystal and umbrella tip

  D. Leather wrap as needed, 1/2" wide

  E. Epoxy glue or weather treatment for leather

Construction:

The standard crystal coupling mount is used on the curved handle. Wrap the 2" long crystal with copper foil tape and glue it into the 3/4" coupling with instant bonding glue. The coupling is then glued onto the curved handle of the umbrella and the leather is spiral-wrapped and glued up to the base of the handle. This is rather like wrapping a curved rod instead of a straight one.

The pointed tip of the umbrella is covered with a 5" long, 1/2" diameter open-ended crystal rod. Wrap the base of the crystal with copper foil tape so that it will fit tightly into the 1/2" diameter copper tubing. Also wrap the pointed tip of the umbrella with the copper foil tape and then glue the copper tubing on the tip making sure it fits tightly. Next wrap and glue the leather on the rod. The leather wrap can be treated with water proofing treatment or coated with an epoxy type glue to seal it against the rain.

CRYSTAL CANES

Crystal canes make excellent walking sticks for hikes in rough country. Imagine the increase in energy, vitality and spiritual awareness you'll feel when you combine fresh air and exercise with the use of crystals. The crystals will probably appreciate the outing too.

Materials:

Double-Headed Cane

   A. Copper coupler, 1/2" diameter

   B. Copper reducer, 3/4" to 1/2" diameter

   C. Two quartz crystals, 1/2" diameter by 1" to 2" long

   D. Copper tape to use for shim around crystals

   E. Instant bonding glue

   F. 1/2" wide leather wrap (optional)

   G. Double-headed cane

Standard Cane

   A. Copper coupler, 3/4" diameter

   B. Quartz crystal, 3/4" diameter by 2" long

   C. Copper tape to use for shim around crystal

   D. Instant bonding glue

   E. 1/2" wide leather wrap (optional)

   F. Standard cane with curved head

Construction:

The crystal attachments for canes use standard crystal coupler mounts. These can be either 3/4" or 1/2" in diameter, depending on the diameter of the head of the cane.

For the double-headed cane, wrap the base of the crystals with copper foil tape to provide a tight fit into the coupler and the reducer, then glue the crystals in place with instant bonding glue. Next, the coupler and reducer are glued on either end of the handle with instant bonding glue. The cane shown in the diagram was then wrapped with leather around the handles and a short ways down the length of the wood.

The standard curved cane usually takes a 3/4" coupler. The crystal is mounted inside the coupler by wrapping a strip of copper foil tape around the base of the crystal and then gluing it into the coupler. The coupler is then glued on the end of the handle. It's not necessary to wrap the handle of the cane with leather wrap, but you can do so if you want to.

Using Your Crystal Cane

Taking your crystals for a walk may provide unexpected benefits. You might find yourself communicating with trees, flowers or animals; you might suddenly get the answer to a difficult question you've been asking. Who knows, maybe you'll just come home feeling better about yourself and life in general. Try it and see what happens. When the cane isn't in use, it also makes a wonderful display piece.

CRYSTAL CANES

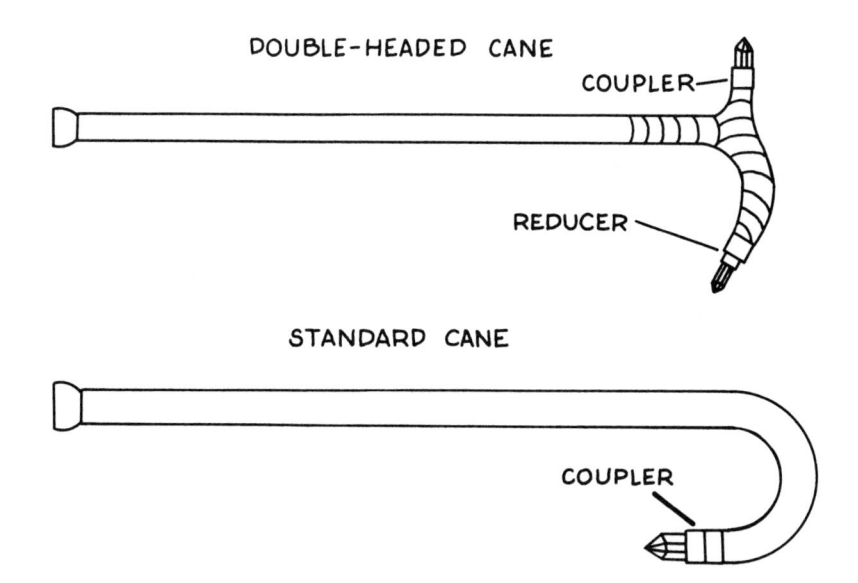

DOUBLE-HEADED CANE
COUPLER
REDUCER

STANDARD CANE
COUPLER

CRYSTAL UMBRELLA

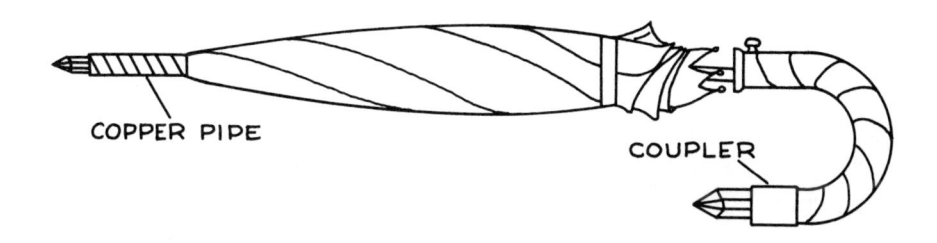

COPPER PIPE
COUPLER

CRYSTAL BULLWHIP

Materials:

A. Leather bullwhip, 6' to 12' length

B. Copper coupling, 1/2" to 1" diameter, depending on diameter of whip

C. Quartz crystal to fit coupler

D. Copper foil tape for shim

E. Instant bonding glue

Construction:

The base of the crystal is wrapped in copper foil to fit the coupling and then glued in the coupling with instant bonding glue. The coupling is glued on the base end of the whip.

CRYSTAL RIDING CROP

Materials:

A. Leather riding crop

B. Copper coupler to fit handle of crop (usually 1/2" in diameter)

C. Quartz crystal to fit coupler

D. Copper foil tape for shim

E. Instant bonding glue

Construction:

Riding crops come in a variety of sizes. Usually a 1/2" coupler can be used. It's also possible to use the copper foil tape as a shim on the base of the crop if the fit isn't perfect.

Wrap the base of the quartz crystal you choose with copper foil tape before gluing the crystal into the coupler. Then simply glue the coupler onto the end of the riding crop or also wrap the handle of the riding crop and then glue the coupler on.

Using your Crystal Bullwhip or Riding Crop

These frivolities are truly that because they pretty well end the usefulness of these items for their original purposes. On the other hand, you might just find better uses for them once the crystals are mounted!

While there may not be too many horsemen or cattlemen interested in these crystal items, they are usually a hit at Halloween parties or as conversation pieces for your wall. They can also be used as you would any power or healing rod. Spiritual development can be fun and entertaining as well as necessary to the maintenance of our planet. Surrounding ourselves with crystals has proved to be of great benefit to our own spiritual development and has helped us to make the most of our potential. They will do the same for you—if you let them.

CRYSTAL BULLWHIP

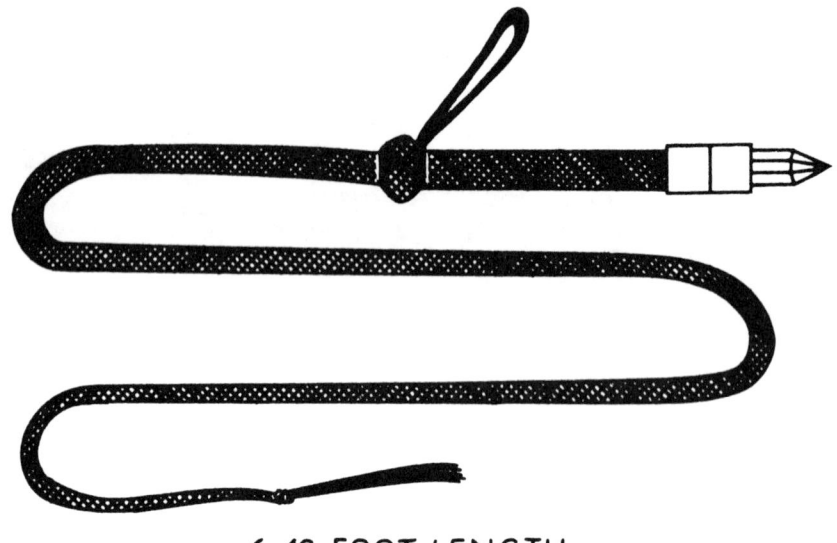

6-12 FOOT LENGTH

CRYSTAL RIDING CROP

27 INCHES

STAY IN TOUCH

On the following pages you will find listed, with their current prices, some of the books and tapes now available on related subjects. Your book dealer stocks most of these, and will stock new titles in the Llewellyn series as they become available. We urge your patronage.

However, to obtain our full catalog, to keep informed of new titles as they are released and to benefit from informative articles and helpful news, you are invited to write for our bimonthly news magazine/catalog, *Llewellyn's New Worlds of Mind and Spirit*. A sample copy is free, and it will continue coming to you at no cost as long as you are an active mail customer. Or you may suscribe for just $7.00 in the U.S.A. and Canada ($20.00 overseas, first class mail). Many bookstores also have *New Worlds* available to their customers. Ask for it.

Stay in touch! In *New Worlds'* pages you will find news and features about new books, tapes and services, announcements of meetings and seminars, articles helpful to our readers, news of authors, products and services, special money-making opportunities, and much more.

Llewellyn's New Worlds of Mind and Spirit
P.O. Box 64383-727, St. Paul, MN 55164-0383, U.S.A.

• • •

TO ORDER BOOKS AND TAPES

If your book dealer does not have the books and tapes described on the following pages readily available, you may order them directly from the publisher by sending full price in U.S. funds, plus $3.00 for postage and handling for orders *under* $10.00; $4.00 for orders *over* $10.00. There are no postage and handling charges for orders over $50.00. Postage and handling rates are subject to change. UPS Delivery: We ship UPS whenever possible. Delivery guaranteed. Provide your street address as UPS does not deliver to P.O. Boxes. UPS to Canada requires a $50.00 minimum order. Allow 4-6 weeks for delivery. Orders outside the U.S.A. and Canada: Airmail—add retail price of book; add $5.00 for each non-book item (tapes, etc.); add $1.00 per item for surface mail.

FOR GROUP STUDY AND PURCHASE

Because there is a great deal of interest in group discussion and study of the subject matter of this book, we feel that we should encourage the adoption and use of this particular book by such groups by offering a special quantity price to group leaders or agents.

Our Special Quantity Price for a minimum order of five copies of *Crystal Warrior* is $29.85 cash-with-order. This price includes postage and handling within the United States. Minnesota residents must add 6.5% sales tax. For additional quantities, please order in multiples of five. For Canadian and foreign orders, add postage and handling charges as above. Credit card (VISA, MasterCard, American Express) orders are accepted. Charge card orders only may be phoned in free ($15.00 minimum order) within the the U.S.A. or Canada by dialing 1-800-THE-MOON. For customer service, call 1-612-291-1970. Mail orders to:

LLEWELLYN PUBLICATIONS
P.O. Box 64383-727 / St. Paul, MN 55164-0383, U.S.A.

Prices subject to change without notice.

CRYSTAL POWER
by Michael G. Smith

This is an amazing book, for what it claims to present—with complete instructions and diagrams so that *you* can work it yourself—is the master technology of ancient Atlantis: psionic devices (mind-controlled and life-energized machines) made from common quartz crystals!

Learn to easily construct an Atlantean power rod that can be used as a weapon or for healing; or a crystal headband stimulating psychic powers; or a time and space communications generator operated purely by your mind.

These crystal devices seem to work only with the disciplined mind power of a human operator, yet their very construction seems to start a process of growth and development, a new evolutionary step in the human psyche that bridges mind and matter.

Does this "re-discovery" mean that we are living, now, in the New Atlantis? Have these power tools been re-invented to meet the needs of this prophetic time? Are psionic machines the culminating power to the people to free us from economic dependence on fossil fuels and smokestack industry? This book answers "yes" to all these questions, and asks you to simply build these devices and put them to work to help bring it all about.

0-87542-725-1, 288 pgs., 5-1/4 x 8, illus. $9.95

CRYSTAL AWARENESS
by Catherine Bowman

For millions of years, crystals have been waiting for people to discover their wonderful powers. Today they are used in watches, computer chips and communication devices. But there is also a spiritual, holistic aspect to crystals.

Crystal Awareness will teach you everything you need to know about crystals to begin working with them. It will also help those who have been working with them to complete their knowledge. Topics include: crystal forms, colored and colorless crystals, single points, clusters and double terminated crystals, crystal and human energy fields, the etheric and spiritual bodies, crystals as energy generators, crystal cleansing and programming, crystal meditation, the value of polished crystals, crystals and personal spiritual growth, crystals and chakras, how to make crystal jewelry, the uses of crystals in the future, color healing, programming crystals with color, compatible crystals and metals, several crystal healing techniques, including the Star of David healing.

Crystal Awareness is destined to be the guide of choice for people who are beginning their investigation of crystals.

0-87542-058-3, 197 pgs., mass market, illus. $3.95

Prices subject to change without notice.

CUNNINGHAM'S ENCYCLOPEDIA OF CRYSTAL, GEM & METAL MAGIC
by Scott Cunningham

Here you will find the most complete information anywhere on the magical qualities of more than 75 crystals and gemstones as well as several metals. The information includes:

- The energy of each gem, crystal or metal
- The planet(s) which rule(s) the crystal, gem or metal
- The magical element associated with the gem, crystal or metal
- The deities associated with each
- The Tarot card associated with each
- The magical powers each crystal, metal and stone is believed to possess

Also included is a complete description of how to use each gemstone, crystal and metal for magical purposes.

This is the book everyone will want to have! This is the book everyone will be quoting. This will be the classic on the subject.

0-87542-126-1, 221 pgs., 6 x 9, illus., 27 color plates $12.95

THE MESSAGE OF THE CRYSTAL SKULL
by Alice Bryant & Phyllis Galde

The crystal skull is the most fascinating, mysterious artifact ever discovered. Thousands of years old, yet it is beyond the capabilities of today's technology to duplicate it. Those who have touched the skull or seen photographs of it claim increased psychic abilities and purification. Read this book and discover how this mystical quartz crystal skull can benefit you and all of humankind. Famed biocrystallographer Frank Dorland shares his research of the skull.

0-87542-092-3, 224 pgs., mass market, illus. $3.95

CRYSTAL HEALING
by Phyllis Galde

Discover the secrets of quartz crystal! Now modern research has shown that crystals have even more healing and therapeutic properties than have been realized. Learn why polished, smoothed crystal is better to use to heighten your intuition, improve creativity and for healing.

Learn to use crystals for reprogramming your subconscious to eliminate problems and negative attitudes that prevent success. Here are techniques—not just theories—that people have successfully used.

This book reveals newly discovered abilities of crystal now accessible to all, and is a sensible approach to crystal use. *Crystal Healing* will be your guide to improve the quality of your life and expand your consciousness.

0-87542-246-2, 224 pgs., mass market, illus. $3.95

Prices subject to change without notice.

THE TRUTH ABOUT CRYSTAL HEALING
by Phyllis Galde

Crystals have been valued throughout history for their healing and energizing qualities. This small book tells you all about them. You will learn historical lore about crystals, how to heal with crystals, the different kinds of crystals, how crystals can enhance your psychic development and the qualities crystal gemstones have. Learn to use the living stones of the Earth for healing, well-being and focusing energy.

0-87542-360-4, 32 pgs., 5-1/2 x 8-1/2 $2.00

THE WOMEN'S BOOK OF HEALING
by Diane Stein

At the front of the women's spirituality movement with her previous books, Diane Stein now helps women (and men) reclaim their natural right to be healers. Included are exercises which can help you to become a healer! Learn about the uses of color, vibration, crystals and gems for healing. Learn about the auric energy field and the chakras.

The book teaches alternative healing theory and techniques and combines them with crystal and gemstone healing, laying on of stones, psychic healing, laying on of hands, chakra work and aura work, and color therapy. It teaches beginning theory in the aura, chakras, colors, creative visualization, meditation, health theory and ethics with some quantum theory. Forty-six gemstones plus clear quartz crystals are discussed in detail, arranged by chakras and colors.

The Women's Book of Healing is designed to teach basic healing (Part I) and healing with crystals and gemstones (Part II). Part I discusses the aura and four bodies, the chakras, basic healing skills of creative visualization, meditation and color work, psychic healing, and laying on of hands. Part II begins with a chapter on clear quartz crystal, then enters gemstone work with introductory gemstone material. The remainder of the book discusses, in chakra by chakra format, specific gemstones for healing work, their properties and uses.

0-87542-759-6, 352 pgs., 6 x 9, illus. $12.95

THE ART OF SPIRITUAL HEALING
by Keith Sherwood

Each of you has the potential to be a healer; to heal yourself and to become a channel for healing others. Healing energy is always flowing through you. Learn how to recognize and tap this incredible energy source. You do not need to be a victim of disease or poor health. Rid yourself of negativity and become a channel for positive healing.

Become acquainted with your three auras and learn how to recognize problems and heal them on a higher level before they become manifested in the physical body as disease.

Special techniques make this book a breakthrough to healing power, but you are also given a concise, easy-to-follow regimen of good health in order to maintain a superior state of being. This is a practical guide to healing.

0-87542-720-0, 256 pgs., 5-1/4 x 8, illus. $7.95

Prices subject to change without notice.

PSYCHIC POWER
by Charles Cosimano

Although popular in many parts of the world, radionics machines have had little application in America, until now that is! Charles Cosimano's book *Psychic Power* introduces these machines to America with a new purpose: to increase your psychic powers.

Using the easy, step-by-step instructions, and for less than a $10.00 investment, you can build a machine which will allow you to read other people's minds, influence their thoughts, communicate with their dreams and be more successful when you do divinations such as working with Tarot cards or pendulums.

For thousands of years, people have looked for an easy, simple and sure way to increase their psychic abilities. Now, the science of psionics allows you to do just that! This book is practical, fun and an excellent source for those wishing to achieve results with etheric energies.

If you just want a book to read, you will find this a wonderful title to excitingly fill a few hours. But if you can spare a few minutes to actually build and use these devices, you will be able to astound yourself and your friends. We are not talking about guessing which numbers will come up on a pair of dice at a mark slightly above average. With practice, you will be able to choose which numbers will come up more often than not! But don't take our word for it. Read the book, build the devices and find out for yourself.

0-87542-097-4, 224 pgs., mass market, illus. $3.95

PSIONIC POWER
by Charles Cosimano

Psionic Power picks up where Cosimano's previous Llewellyn title, *Psychic Power*, left off. This new book takes a giant leap forward in the technology of psychic power, and introduces the most powerful radionic devices yet devised.

Although written specifically to guide the radionics veteran onward, *Psionic Power* still serves as a complete guide to the beginner. The author's light and witty style makes high-tech psionics easy and inviting, giving everyone the chance to expand natural psychic ability with much less work than is normally required in other schools of psychic training.

You will learn detailed techniques for projecting psychic power and defending against psychic attack. New devices are diagrammed and explained, and the author includes an informative section on the use of magical sigils with psionic devices. This is the best book yet written on psionics—the final frontier of the New Age!

0-87542-096-6, 224 pgs., mass market, illus. $3.95

THE LLEWELLYN PRACTICAL GUIDE TO PSYCHIC SELF-DEFENSE AND WELL-BEING
by Denning & Phillips

Psychic well-being and psychic self-defense are two sides of the same coin—just as physical health and resistance to disease are. Each person (and every living thing) is surrounded by an electromagnetic force field, or aura, that can provide the means to psychic self-defense and to dynamic well-being. This book explores the world of very real "psychic warfare" of which we all are victims.

FACT: Every person in our modern world is subjected to psychic stress and psychological bombardment—advertising promotions that play upon primitive emotions, political and religious appeals that work on feelings of insecurity and guilt, noise, threats of violence and war, news of crime and disaster, etc.

This book shows the nature of genuine psychic attacks—ranging from actual acts of black magic to bitter jealousy and hate—and the reality of psychic stress, the structure of the psyche and its interrelationship with the physical body. It shows how each person must develop his weakened aura into a powerful defense-shield—thereby gaining both physical protection and energetic well-being that can extend to protection from physical violence, accidents ... even ill-health.

This book gives exact instructions for the fortification of the aura, specific techniques for protection, and the Rite of the First Kathisma using the Psalms to invoke Divine Blessing. Illustrated with "puts-you-in-the-picture" drawings, and includes powerful techniques not only for your personal use but for group use.
0-87542-190-3, 306 pgs., 5-1/4 x 8, illus. $8.95

THE LLEWELLYN PRACTICAL GUIDE TO THE DEVELOPMENT OF PSYCHIC POWERS
by Denning & Phillips

You may not realize it, but you already have the ability to use ESP, astral vision and clairvoyance, divination, dowsing, prophecy, communication with spirits, to exercise (as with any talent) and develop them.

Written by two of the most knowledgeable experts in the world of Magick today, this book is a complete course—teaching you, step-by-step, how to develop these powers that actually have been yours since birth. Using the techniques they teach, you will soon be able to move objects at a distance, see into the future, know the thoughts and feelings of another person, find lost objects, locate water and even people using your own no-longer latent talents.

Psychic powers are as much a natural ability as any other talent. You'll learn to play with these new skills, work with groups of friends to accomplish things you never would have believed possible before reading this book. The text shows you how to make the equipment you can use, the exercises you can do—many of them at any time, anywhere—and how to use your abilities to change your life and the lives of those close to you. Many of the exercises are presented in forms that can be adapted as games for pleasure and fun, as well as development.
0-87542-191-1, 256 pgs., 5-1/4 x 8, illus. $8.95

Prices subject to change without notice.

CHIRON
by Barbara Hand Clow

This book is about the most recently discovered planet, Chiron. This little-known planet was first sighted in 1977. It has an eccentric orbit: on a 50-51 year cycle between Saturn and Uranus. It brought farsightedness into astrology because Chiron is the bridge to the outer planets, Neptune and Pluto, from the inner ones.

The small but influential planet of Chiron reveals how the New Age initiation will affect each one of us. Chiron is an initiator, an alchemist, a healer, and a spiritual guide. For those who are astrologers, *Chiron* has more information than any other book about this planet. Learn why Chiron rules Virgo and the Sixth House. Have the necessary information about Chiron in each house, in each sign, and how the aspects affect each person's chart.

Chiron is sure to become a best-selling, albeit controversial, book in the astrological world. The influences of Chiron are an important new factor in understanding capabilities and potentials which we all have. Chiron rules: healing with the hands, healing with crystals, initiation and alchemy and alteration of the body by mind and spirit. Chiron also rules cartomancy and the Tarot reader. As such it is an especially vital resource for everyone who uses the Tarot.

0-87542-094-X, 320 pgs., 6 x 9, charts $9.95

LIFE FORCE
by Leo Ludzia

A secret living energy—as ancient as the pyramids, as modern as Star Wars. Since the beginning of time, certain people have known that there is this energy—a power that can be used by people for healing, magick, and spiritual development. It's been called many names: mana, orgone, psionic, prana, kundalini, odic, chi and others.

Leo Ludzia puts it all together in this amazing book. This is the first book which shows the histories and compares the theories and methods of using this marvelous energy. This force is available to us all, if only we know how to tap into it. Ludzia shows you how to make devices which will help you better use and generate this Life Force. This specialized information includes easy-to-follow-directions on: how to build and use pyramids, orgone generators such as those used by Wilhelm Reich, and how to make and use the "black box" designed and used by the genius inventor T.G. Hieronymus.

Unlike some New Age books, this is a title that will appeal to everyone! Scientists, psychics, occultists and mystics of Eastern and Western paths will want to read this book. It will also attract those people who are interested in psionics, radionics, UFOs and fortean phenomena.

0-87542-437-6, 192 pgs., mass market, illus. $3.95

Prices subject to change without notice.

SHAMANISM AND THE MYSTERY LINES
by Paul Devereux

This book will take you across archaic landscapes, into contact with spiritual traditions as old as the human central nervous system and into the deepest recesses of the human psyche. Explore the mystery surrounding "ley lines": stone rows, prehistoric linear earthwork, and straight tracks in archaic landscapes around the world. Why would the ancients, without the wheel or horse, want such broad and exact roads? Why the apparent obsession with straightness? Why the parallel sections?

Are they energy lines? Traders' tracks? For those who have definite ideas as to what a ley line is, be prepared for a surprise ... and a possible shift in your beliefs about this intriguing phenomenon.

The theory put forth and proved in *Shamanism and the Mystery Lines* is startling: that all ancient landscape lines—whether physical manifestations as created by the Amerindians or conceptual as in the case of Feng shui—are in essence spirit lines. And underlying the concept of spirit and straightness is a deep, universal experience yielded by the human central nervous system: that of shamanic magical flight—or the out-of-body experience. This explanation is as simple and direct as the lines themselves ... flight is the straight way over land.

0-87542-189-X, 240 pgs., 6 x 9, illus. $12.95

SHAMANISM AND THE ESOTERIC TRADITION
by Anelique S. Cook & G.A. Hawk

Recharge and enhance your magical practice by returning to the *source* of the entire esoteric tradition—the shamanism of the ancient hunters and gatherers.

Whether you're involved in yoga, divination, Witchcraft or ritual magic, *Shamanism and the Esoteric Tradition* introduces you to the fundamental neo-shamanic techniques that produce immediate results. Shamanic practice is a tremendous aid in self-healing and personal growth. It also produces euphoria by releasing beta-endorphins, an effective antidote against depression.

The enormously powerful techniques presented here include inner journeys to find a power animal and teacher, past-life regression, healing methods, and journeys to help the dead. Gradually and properly used, shamanic power helps you generate positive synchronicities that can alter so-called "chance" life events, and enhance personal satisfaction, freedom and wholeness.

0-87542-325-6, 240 pgs., 6 x 9, illus. $12.95

Prices subject to change without notice.